THE SOUL OF THE STRANGER

Joy Ladin

THE SOUL OF THE STRANGER

READING GOD AND TORAH FROM A TRANSGENDER PERSPECTIVE

Brandeis University Press   Waltham, Massachusetts

Brandeis University Press
An imprint of University Press of New England
www.upne.com
© 2019 Brandeis University
All rights reserved
Manufactured in the United States of America
Designed by Mindy Basinger Hill
Typeset in Minion Pro

The HBI Series on Jewish Women is supported
by a generous gift from Dr. Laura S. Schor.

For permission to reproduce any of the material in this book,
contact Permissions, University Press of New England, One Court Street, Suite 250,
Lebanon NH 03766; or visit www.upne.com.

Library of Congress Cataloging-in-Publication Data
Names: Ladin, Joy, 1961– author.
Title: The soul of the stranger : reading God and Torah from a transgender
     perspective / Joy Ladin.
Description: Waltham, Massachusetts : Brandeis University Press, [2019] |
     Series: HBI series on Jewish women | Includes bibliographical references and index.
Identifiers: LCCN 2018024055 (print) | LCCN 2018033753 (ebook) | ISBN 9781512602944
     (epub, pdf, & mobi) | ISBN 9781512600667 (cloth : alk. paper) | ISBN 9781512602937
     (pbk. : alk. paper)
Subjects: LCSH: God (Judaism)—Attributes. | God (Judaism)—Knowableness. | Gender identity
     in the Bible. | Gender nonconformity—Religious aspects—Judaism. | Bible—Transgender
     interpretations. | Jewish transgender people—Religious life—United States. | Transgender
     people—Religious life—United States. | Ladin, Joy, 1961–
Classification: LCC BM610 (ebook) | LCC BM610 .L334 2019 (print) | DDC 296.3086/7—dc23
LC record available at https://lccn.loc.gov/2018024055

5   4   3   2   1

For Nancy Mayer,
without whom
neither this book
nor my life
would have
been possible,
and for You,
my favorite
stranger

CONTENTS

ACKNOWLEDGMENTS

The writing of this book was supported by fellowships from the National Endowment for the Arts and the Hadassah Brandeis Institute, and a sabbatical semester funded by Yeshiva University.

From beginning to end, Nancy Mayer has been my guide. Without her, many parts of this book would not have been written, because without her, it wouldn't have occurred to me to write them.

I would never have dared write a book about the Torah without the encouragement of Rabbi Burton Visotzky of the Jewish Theological Seminary, whose generous critique of an early draft transformed my conception of what I was writing and to whom I was writing.

As always, Liz Denlinger made my writing better, sharper, and more concise, patiently reminding me that saying the truth clearly once is always better than waving vaguely toward it seven or eight times.

I am also grateful to Steven Philp for his invaluable assistance with traditional Jewish sources and citations.

This book grew out of many talks I have given and essays I have published over the past six or seven years. Though my ideas and language changed substantially as the book took shape, I drew particularly on the following essays, and gratefully acknowledge the support of the following publications:

Tikkun, which published "The Genesis of Gender," "Once Out of Nature: Reflections on Body, Soul, Gender and God," and "Both Wilderness and Promised Land: How Torah Grows When Read Through LGBTQ Eyes"; "The Stolen Blessing" appeared on the *Tikkun* blog.

Lilith, which published "Standing Again at Sinai, Again: Jewish Feminism and Transgender Jews."

Keshet blog, which posted "Passover: Festival of Binaries," "Shipwrecked with God," and "Transgendered Hearts: Abraham, Sarah, and Isaac."

The Human Rights Campaign blog, which posted "Reading Between the Angels: How Torah Speaks to Transgender Jews."

THE SOUL OF THE STRANGER

SHIPWRECKED WITH GOD

I'm often asked how I reconcile being religious with being transgender. For me, there has never been a conflict between them. For as long as I can remember, I felt that I was female, and for as long as I can remember, I have sensed God's presence.

I've become used to talking about being transgender, but no matter how much I talk about my relationship with God, it still makes me squirm to say, "I feel God's presence." I grew up surrounded by people for whom God is "God," an empty word, an outdated superstition, a target for rage about the Holocaust and other tragedies, a symbol of ideals that human beings find hard to live up to. Even at Hebrew school and synagogue, I dared not let anyone guess that, to me, God was not an abstraction but someone who was there, invisible but as real as cold or warmth or humidity.

No one else I knew seemed to experience God as a living presence. But when I read the Torah—the Hebrew Bible, what Christians call "the Old Testament"—that was the God I found there. The Torah portrays God as passionately involved with human lives—not just with extraordinary individuals like Abraham and Sarah, but with everyone. God doesn't buy or sell, but insists that human beings do so honestly. God doesn't have parents, but is concerned about how we treat ours. God doesn't live in space or time, is not subject to famine or plenty, day or night, birth or death, but wants us to give meaning to the seasons and places of our lives.

But the Torah also makes it clear that although God is present and personally involved in human lives, God is not human. God has no face, no form, no beginning or end, and can't be understood in any of the terms we use to understand ourselves and our world. As God tells Moses at the burning bush, God is what God is, and will be what God will be (Exod. 3:14).

This invisible, incomprehensible, but undeniably present God is the God I grew up with, not because my family was religious (they weren't), not because we read the Torah together (we didn't), not because religious teachers or leaders taught me to think of God this way (they didn't teach me to think about God at all), but because, for as long as I can remember, this was the God to whom I woke and with whom I fell asleep, the God to whom I whispered and whimpered, pleaded, and sometimes screamed.

To me, God was not a mystical experience; God was a fact of life, like my parents. But I felt closer to God than to my parents. My parents, like other human beings, identified me with my male body. To them, I was a boy named Jay, and both because I loved them and because I was terrified of being rejected if they guessed the truth, I did my best to act like the boy they thought I was.

God never mistook me for the body others saw. God knew who I truly was, and understood how alone I felt, because God, like me, had no body to make God visible, no face human beings could see.

Unlike God, apart from gender, I wasn't so different from the kids I grew up with. Like other children, I ate and slept and went to school, rode my bike, played, was self-centered and sometimes cruel, careless of the truth and others' feelings. Even though I knew that the way I looked on the outside didn't express who I was on the inside, I still judged others by the color of their skin, the fitness of their bodies, and the shabbiness or sharpness of their clothes, and assumed that, unlike me, other people really were the boys or girls, men or women, they appeared to be.

But despite the many ways I was like other children, I always felt I was something else, something that had no name or place in the world. Nowadays, I would say that because I didn't fit into the gender binary that defines everyone as either male or female, I couldn't feel that I was really part of humanity. But when I was child, all I knew was that my sense of being female made me different in ways that were shameful and danger-ous, ways that kept others from seeing or understanding or loving me. Present but invisible, I felt like a ghost, hidden within and haunting the boy everyone thought I was.

Of course, none of us is exactly who we seem to be. Few people old enough to think about it would say that their bodies perfectly express who they are, or that they always feel and act in ways that fit others' ideas of who they ought to be. Gender and other identities are always compromises that require each of us to sacrifice some of our messy individuality in order to fit into our families, friendships, and communities.

But when it came to gender, I couldn't make that compromise. I could, and did, act like the boy I was supposed to be, but I couldn't feel that I was really that boy, couldn't identify myself with other boys, couldn't feel I was really present in any relationship, because every relationship was based on gender. I wasn't just my parents' child; I was supposed to be their son. I wasn't just a kid on the block; I was supposed to be one of the boys. I wasn't just a Jew; I was supposed to be a Jewish male. And so, even though I was surrounded by people who thought they knew me, I grew up feeling invisible, afraid, and alone.

But I was alone with God. All the things that cut me off from other people—my lack of a body that felt like mine, my inability to fit into gender categories, my sense of being utterly, unspeakably different—made me feel closer to God. God knew who and what I was. God had created me, fitting my mismatched body and soul together. God was always there, day and night, as I tried to live and sometimes tried to die. We were an odd couple, me struggling with a body that didn't feel like mine, God existing beyond all that is, was, and will be. But when it came to relating to human beings, God and I had something in common: neither of us could be seen or understood by those we dwelt among and loved.

And so, for as long as I can remember, being transgender has brought me closer to God. That may seem strange. Both religious and nonreligious people tend to think of transgender identities as inherently secular. But there are many religious people whose relationships with God have been profoundly shaped by being transgender because, as they wrestled with suffering, isolation, and questions about who they were and how they should live, they, like other religious people, turned to God for the understanding they couldn't find among human beings.

Most religious traditions recognize that conditions that cut us off from other people can bring us closer to God. But if I had I told my rabbi or Hebrew school teachers or parents or community leaders that God and I regularly commiserated about the difficulties of loving people who couldn't see or understand us, they would, no doubt, have let me know that the Creator of the Universe is not in the habit of talking with children, and certainly not with children who don't fit into the categories of male or female. Though there is much more awareness of transgender people today than when I was growing up, and more religious communities that accept openly transgender members, even the most welcoming communities have just begun to consider how religious traditions based on the assumption that human beings are either and always male or female can speak to people who don't fit those categories.

I was in my mid-forties before I knew any rabbis who would accept me as a transgender Jew, but I heard Jewish tradition speak to my life every Yom Kippur afternoon, when Jews traditionally read the Book of Jonah, which tells a story every transgender person knows: the story of someone desperate to avoid living as the person (in Jonah's case, as the prophet) they know themselves to be.

From the beginning of the book, when God orders him to "Go at once to Nineveh . . . and proclaim judgment upon it; for their wickedness has come before Me," Jonah knows he is a prophet (Jon. 1:2). Jonah doesn't ask why God chose him to deliver this message, or argue, as Moses does at the burning bush, that he isn't qualified to do so. He just runs away, because, as he explains in the final chapter, he knows God won't destroy Nineveh, no matter how wicked the people are: "That is why I fled . . . I know that You are a compassionate and gracious God, slow to anger, abounding in kindness, renouncing punishment" (4:2). Even as God tells him of God's impending judgment, Jonah, as befits a prophet, already knows that God will spare them.

Jonah is so desperate to avoid being a prophet that he abandons whatever life he has been living and boards a ship to Tarshish. But as many transgender people know, when we flee from being who we are, we flee from life itself. While his ship is tossed by a God-sent storm, Jonah stays asleep in the hold of the heaving ship, in a slumber so deep that it overrides even his instinct for self-preservation. When the captain wakes him and tells him to "call upon your god" for deliverance, Jonah responds not with prayer but with a suicidal gesture, telling the sailors, "Heave me overboard, and the sea will calm down for you" (1:6, 12).

Why would Jonah respond this way? God sent the storm because he refused to go to Nineveh, so it would have made sense for Jonah to appease

God's anger by telling God he would do what God ordered him to do. Jonah's self-destructive response reflects a psychological pattern that is all too familiar among transgender people: flee from yourself for as long as you can, and when you can no longer endure the internal and external storms, kill yourself for the sake of others, so you can avoid ever having to live as who you are. Jonah may have thought he was killing himself for the sake of the sailors, but the truth is that he is so desperate to avoid living as the prophet he is that he prefers not to live at all.

Transgender people often tell ourselves that suicide will resolve the conflict between our need to be, and not be, who we truly are. Our families, our communities, and our world will be better off without us, we think, and we, released from the shame of hiding and the terror of living as who we are, will finally be at peace. In Jonah's case, this suicidal fantasy seems to come true: when Jonah is thrown overboard, the sea stops raging, and he sinks peacefully "into the depths, into the heart of the sea," where he is "swallowed" by a "huge fish" (1:15, 2:3).

But Jonah, miraculously, doesn't die. In the depths of the sea, in the belly of the fish, Jonah finds himself alone with the God he fled. God literally surrounds him, providing him with breath, warmth, and protection, sustaining his life in the midst of death.

In other words, Jonah's flight from himself leads him simultaneously closer to death and closer to God. That spiritual paradox is at the heart of his story, and it was at the heart of the story of my life when I was living as a man I knew I wasn't. Like Jonah, I was so desperate to avoid living as who I was that I eagerly chose death over life, despair over hope, isolation over human connection. Even in the midst of family and friends, I felt like I was alone at the bottom of the ocean. But I wasn't alone: though suicidal depression swallowed me for decades, God was there, surrounding me, holding me, keeping me alive.

Even while Jonah is in the belly of the fish, he sees his miraculous deliverance as a turning point: "I sank to the base of the mountains; the bars of the earth closed upon me forever; yet You brought my life up from the pit, O LORD my God!" (2:7). Jonah is so grateful that God has saved him that when the fish vomits him out on shore, he overcomes his reluctance to present himself as a prophet and heads to Nineveh.

Unlike Jonah, I experienced God as preserving me in the depths rather than delivering me to life. God didn't want me to live as who I really was, I told myself. God wanted me—and was helping me—to submerge my true self forever. That's what love is, I told myself: pretending to be what others want you to be. Suffering in silence. Embracing loneliness. Giving up on joy.

Year after year, when the ram's horn blew on Yom Kippur, the Day of Atonement, I wept, not because I was repenting of my sins, but because I knew that no matter how heartfelt my confessions, as long as I lived as a man, I would never feel grateful, or even truly alive. God could preserve my life in the depths of suicidal despair, but even God couldn't deliver me from those depths until I did what Jonah did: accept that I had to live as who I truly was.

Despite his gratitude for God's deliverance, Jonah still isn't thrilled about being a prophet, which in his case means walking through Nineveh proclaiming, "Forty days more, and Nineveh shall be overthrown!" (3:4). As Jonah no doubt knew, prophets often paid a heavy price for expressing God's displeasure with the social order. Jeremiah was thrown into a pit; four hundred of Elijah's fellow prophets were murdered. Though Jonah isn't imprisoned or killed, his work as a prophet requires him to disrupt the community and challenge social norms by acting in ways that call unseemly attention to himself.

Like Jonah, I knew that I couldn't live as who I was without being stared at, treated as an embarrassment or public menace, and risking the ridicule and violence that transgender people face every day. It was easy to imagine how I and those I loved might suffer if I dared to express my female gender identity, but what good, I wondered, could possibly come of living a truth that would mark me, publicly and permanently, as "other"?

That is Jonah's question, too. Despite his firsthand knowledge of God's plans, Jonah never understands what good comes of him living as a prophet, because, as he says at the end of the book, he always knew that God would be merciful whether or not he marched through Nineveh proclaiming that the city was going to be destroyed. But unlike Jonah, the people of Nineveh couldn't hear God summoning them to change their lives. They needed to hear that message from a human throat, from a body they could see, from a person who not only saw things differently than they did but who was also willing to stand up, and stand out, as different. Jonah saved Nineveh—or rather, enabled Nineveh to save itself—by accepting the discomfort and the risk of being the prophet he was.

Most transgender people aren't leaders, visionaries, or prophets. Some day, being transgender will be no harder to understand or accept than other ways of being human. When that day comes, we won't have to wonder whether we should kill ourselves for the sake of others, or pretend to be other than who we are. We will face our human share of sorrow and struggle, and when we look to religious communities for help, we will know that the traditions that sustain, comfort, and guide others are there to sustain, comfort, and guide us, too.

But for most of us, that future is still a distant dream, and so transgender people daily face the kinds of choices Jonah faced: will we run away, sink into despair, throw ourselves into the sea, or will we live as who we are, even when that means being seen as different, disruptive, or a threat to social order?

I don't mean to suggest that the Book of Jonah is about being transgender. The Book of Jonah is about being human. But transgender experience is human experience, and questions transgender people face are questions that we all face. Everyone, transgender or not, has to decide what parts of ourselves we will and will not live. Each of us has to decide when we can't and when we must sacrifice our individuality for the sake of our families and communities, when we have to be what others count on us to be, and when, like Jonah, we have to live the truths that set us apart from others and reveal to the world what we have only revealed to God. When we read the Book of Jonah in the light of transgender experience, we are reminded that the crisis it dramatizes is one that most people face sooner or later: the crisis of realizing that we must live what makes us different, or we cannot live at all.

As I hope this reading and other readings in this book show, religious traditions based on the assumption that everyone is simply male or female can and do speak to the lives of those who do not fit binary gender categories—which means that religious communities can include openly transgender people without abandoning or betraying those traditions. Every religious community that embraces people who don't make sense in terms of binary gender categories honors the image of the incomprehensible God in which, the first chapter of Genesis tells us, all human beings are created. In fact, if we take seriously the idea that human beings are created in the image of God, then whenever we expand our understanding of humanity, we can expand our understanding of God.[1]

Religious traditions based on the Torah tend to think of humanity in terms of men. The Torah is filled with stories about men and laws directed toward men, and the assumption that male experience is the most important aspect of human experience shapes the way God is portrayed. Though the Torah doesn't portray God as a man, the Torah uses male pronouns to refer to God. When God talks to individuals, they are almost always men. When God is glorified in song, most of the metaphors used—"king," "warrior," "father," and so on—are based on male figures and experience. Because humanity is largely conceived in terms of men, so is God.

As Judith Plaskow and other feminist theologians have argued, when we expand our idea of humanity to give as much attention to women as to men, we expand the aspects of human experience we can draw on to understand God. We can understand God as female as well as male, mother as well as father, queen as well as king, nurturer as well as warrior, "She" as well as "He." God, of course, is no more female than male, but thinking of God in terms of women's as well as men's experience draws attention to aspects of God we tend to overlook otherwise.

Male-centered and feminist theologies draw our attention to ways in which God can be understood by analogy to human maleness and femaleness. By extension, expanding our definition of humanity to include transgender people draws our attention to ways in which God can be understood by analogy to transgender lives—the lives of those who, like God, do not fit traditional roles and categories.[2]

But when I started reading the Torah as a child, I was struck more by how its stories of God resonated with my life than by how my life could help me understand God. This was the 1960s. There was no Laverne Cox, no Caitlyn Jenner, no internet blogs or discussion boards. The Torah's stories about God were the first I had seen about someone who, like me, didn't fit binary gender categories, someone who didn't have a body to make them visible, someone who had no place in the human world.

Although my reading of the Torah has always been shaped by my experience of being someone who doesn't make sense in terms of binary gender, I haven't always read it from a transgender perspective. For most of my life, I didn't think of myself as "transgender," a word I didn't learn until my mid-forties. I thought of myself as a "transsexual," a medical term coined to refer to people born into bodies of one sex who identify so strongly with the other that they feel the need to change themselves and live as the opposite gender. I didn't see "transsexual" as an identity I embraced and shared with others. I saw it as a life-threatening condition I had to live with, receive treatment for, and someday, I hoped, be cured of and leave behind, so that I could live as a woman.

When I started writing this book, I realized that I wanted to read the Torah from a transgender rather than a transsexual perspective. My sense of kinship with the God I saw in the Torah didn't grow out of feeling female despite having a male body; it grew out of my more general experience of not fitting into a world in which it is assumed that everyone is either and always male or female. That's what "transgender" means in this book: having a sense of self that does not fit the traditional binary gender categories of male and female.[3]

Of course, there is no such thing as a general or universal transgender perspective. "Transgender" is a catchall term that gathers together many kinds of people who don't fit binary gender categories, people with very different relations to gender and identity. Some transgender people identify as both male and female; some don't identify as either. Some look forward to a day when everyone will accept any gender an individual expresses; some hope for a world in which gender is no longer important, or doesn't exist at all. To make things even more complicated, the terms for people who don't identify as simply male or female are changing all the time. It's possible that a few years from now the word "transgender" will seem as dated as the term "transsexual" sounds to many college students today.

The readings of the Torah I offer in this book reflect my particular transgender perspective, which has been shaped by many factors, including growing up white, middle class, and ethnically but not religiously Jewish in upstate New York in the 1960s and 1970s. As my experience and understanding of being transgender (and being human) have changed over the course of my life, so has the way I read the Torah.

Although my readings grow out of my personal experience, I don't mean this book to be memoir or spiritual autobiography. When I write about my own life, my goal is to offer specific examples of transgender experience that I know some (not all) trans people share. Similarly, my goal in offering readings of the Torah is not to explain how I personally read the text, but to suggest how the Torah may speak to and be illuminated by trans perspectives and lives.

It may seem wrong to some people to read the Torah from this perspective. After all, though there have always been human beings and human bodies that do not fit binary gender categories, the ideas about gender, identity, and humanity implied by the word "transgender" are recent inventions. But according to Jewish tradition, there is nothing wrong with reading the Torah in terms of ideas and perspectives that arose after the Torah was written. As Barry Holtz explains in *Back to the Sources: Reading the Classic Jewish Texts*, the ancient rabbis who wrestled with the Torah's meaning after the destruction of the Second Temple saw the Torah as including not just the text itself but all future interpretations of it:

> [T]he assumption in rabbinic thought is always that new interpretation is implied by the Torah itself. . . . Torah, to the rabbis, was an *eternally relevant book because it was written* (dictated, inspired—it doesn't matter) *by a perfect Author*, an Author who intended it to be eternal. . . . The rabbis could not help but believe that this wondrous and sacred text, the Torah, was intended for all Jews and for all times. Surely God could foresee the need for new interpretations; all interpretations, therefore, are already in the Torah text.[4]

In other words, the Torah's later readers are simply discovering meaning that, according to the rabbis, God has planted in its words.

To those who see the Torah as a human document, written by, for, and in the language of ancient Israelites, the idea that the Torah includes every interpretation of it will probably seem absurd. But to the rabbis, as to many traditionally religious readers, the Torah is more than a human document: it is God's word, human language imbued with God's divine perspective.

If the rabbis are right, it is not heretical to claim that the Torah speaks to transgender lives and concerns, or to suggest that reading the Torah from trans perspectives can uncover its truths; it is deeply traditional. Indeed, to say otherwise is to read the Torah as merely human language, as language that speaks from and to limited human perspectives, rather than as divine language that speaks to each reader across time, space, and culture.

In reading the Torah from a transgender perspective, I am not trying to "queer," "trans," or otherwise reimagine the text. Like the rabbis, I believe that all interpretations, including those from this perspective, are already planted in the Torah, waiting for us to discover them, and like the rabbis, I believe that new interpretations add to rather than compete with traditional understandings. It is not my intention to show how the Torah should be read by trans or non-trans people. My hope is that these readings will help bridge the chasm that too often yawns between transgender people and religious communities by suggesting ways in which reading from a transgender perspective can grow out of and contribute to religious tradition, and that the Torah and transgender lives can speak to and illuminate one another. To those ends, I have tried to hold the readings of the Torah I offer to the following standards:

1. They must be grounded in what Jewish tradition calls the *pshat*, the plain sense of the text.
2. They must be true to me personally: true to the way I read the text; true to my relationship with God; and true to my experience of being transgender.[5]
3. They must not just be true to me: they must also be true to aspects of transgender or religious experience that I share with others.
4. They must acknowledge the ways in which my understanding of the Torah has changed as my situation, experience, and understanding of myself as a trans person have changed.
5. They must acknowledge the tensions, conflicts, and contradictions among transgender perspectives, the plain text of

the Torah, and the traditions that have grown out of that text. Rather than avoiding or pretending to resolve such problems, they must describe and consider them.

Instead of presenting an overarching argument, each chapter of this book explores questions raised by reading the Torah from a transgender perspective.

I begin by exploring a question that often arises in debates about whether religious traditions can include people who are not simply male or female: how can we reconcile transgender identities with the opening of Genesis, in which God, by creating human beings male and female, seems to build binary gender into the definition of humanity? Chapter 1, "The Genesis of Gender," examines God's relationship to gender and the gender binary by looking closely at the role gender plays in God's creation of humanity in the first three chapters of Genesis. These chapters present gender not as a divine decree but as a human invention, a means by which human beings identify and relate to one another that changes over time.

Even though Genesis doesn't say that God created the gender binary, the only adults we see in the Torah are men who were born male and women who were born female. Does the Torah allow for the possibility that people may not fit the gender roles they were born to, that some of us may become something other than the men and women our families and societies believe we should be? I explore this question in chapter 2, "Trans Experience in the Torah," by examining stories in Genesis about Abraham, Sarah, and Jacob that center on how their gender roles are transformed by their relationships with God. Although God does not change their sex, God gives each of them the trans experience of becoming people who violate traditional ideas of what men and women should be by, for example, ordering Abraham to abandon his firstborn role of caring for his elderly father, making Sarah a new mother in old age, and requiring Jacob to steal his firstborn brother Esau's blessing to fulfill his spiritual destiny. In these stories, the Torah not only allows for the possibility that people may not fit their assigned gender roles; it connects the trans experience of violating gender roles to intimacy with God.

But these stories do not suggest what trans experience has to do with relating to God. I explore that question in chapter 3, "Close Encounters with an Incomprehensible God." Here I read God's efforts to relate to people even though God does not make sense in human terms in light of my struggles to relate to other human beings as someone who does not make sense in terms of binary gender. Before my gender transition, I felt that being transgender brought me closer to God because I, like God, was invisible and incomprehensible to those around me. These trans experiences helped me understand the scenes in the Torah in which God struggles to relate to and be recognized by human beings. But when God interacts with Abraham and Moses, God finds ways to relate to and be recognized by them despite being invisible and incomprehensible. Reading those interactions in light of my post-transition experiences of relating to others as someone who is openly transgender highlights the difficulties God and human beings face in relating to one another, and suggests how, in the Torah and out, we can negotiate them.

Trans experiences can speak to the Torah's stories about God's efforts to relate to human beings because anyone, even God, who does not fit human roles and categories will face similar social problems in human relationships. But the Torah is not just stories about God. Much of it is devoted to laws based on the gender binary assumption that human beings are always and only male or female. How can the Torah speak to the lives and concerns of transgender people when so many of its laws are based on binary gender? I explore this question in chapter 4, "Reading between the Binaries," by comparing ideas about gender and identity we find in the Torah's laws to the ways in which gender and identity figure in the lives of transgender people today.

Although much has changed since biblical times, in many ways, the power given to the gender binary in the Torah's laws is surprisingly similar to the power the gender binary has in the contemporary United States. For example, the U.S. census and the Levite census commanded in Numbers both require that human beings be identified as either male or female based on their biological sex, instead of treating gender as self-determined by individuals—an idea that is the basis for transgender identities. But though the Torah's laws don't recognize gender as self-determined, the laws of Nazirite vows empower people to change their behavior and appearance in ways that, like gender transition, violate social norms, mark them as different, and set them apart from those around them. And though the Torah uses binary, either-or language to describe not only gender but also Israelite identity, even the laws of Passover, the festival God founds to define and celebrate Israelite identity, include exceptions that recognize that human lives are too messy and complicated to fit binary terms. The recognition that human beings can never be fully described in binary terms is the basis for transgender identities and lives, and God's acknowledgment of it in the laws of Passover lays the basis for even the most traditional religious communities to accept members who do not fit binary gender categories.

Even when we recognize how religious traditions and transgender lives can speak to and illuminate one another, it can still be hard for traditional religious communities to include transgender members, because so many traditional practices, roles, and relationships are based on the assumption that everyone is either and always male or female.[6] Although some traditional religious communities are working to include openly transgender people, others see accommodating trans members as disruptive, disrespectful of tradition, and a distraction from, if not a threat to, the communal worship. What, if anything, does the work of including openly trans people have to do with what the Torah portrays as the fundamental work of religious community—making a place for God in our midst? I explore this question in chapter 5, "Knowing the Soul of the Stranger," by examining the Torah's portrayals of God's difficulty in finding a place in the Israelite community and the Israelites' difficulties in accommodating the God who dwells among them, and comparing them with the difficulties faced by transgender people and others who are seen as too different to fit in or be seen as "one of us."

People who come out as trans in traditional religious communities are often treated as strangers, even by those who have known them all their lives, because they no longer act in ways that make sense in terms of binary gender. Similarly, the human rebellions and divine rages recorded in the Book of Numbers make it clear that even after decades of wandering with God in their midst, to the Israelites, God remains a stranger, a deity whose feelings and actions make no sense to them. Perhaps that is why God repeatedly commands the Israelites to accommodate and include "the stranger who dwells among you," the non-Israelite who embraces the Israelite community as home. For God, the inclusion of those we see as different is not a disruption or a distraction for religious communities; it is an essential religious practice, part of making a place for the ultimate stranger, God.

———

The questions I explore in this book have shaped my relationship to the Torah from the time I was a child, growing within me as I have grown, summoning me to recognize and honor my kinship with humanity and God. After Jews read from the Torah in synagogue, we sing a verse from Proverbs affirming that we see the Torah as "a tree of life" (Prov. 3:18). To me, the Torah is not just a tree of life in general—it is the tree of *my* life. Through the terror and loneliness of being a child without a body, to the isolation and despair of living for decades as a man I knew I wasn't, to the daily miracle of waking as my still unfinished self, I have clung to that tree, knowing the Torah is holding me, speaking to me, reminding me that my life, like the lives of my ancestors, is a day that God has made, a tiny incomprehensible expression of the vast incomprehensible God who incomprehensibly created each of us.

ONE

THE GENESIS OF GENDER

But We Need the Eggs

In the beginning, there was gender. We all were born into a world in which to be human is to be divided by gender, assigned roles based on gender, taught to understand ourselves and our relationships with others in terms of gender. We inherited this world from our parents, who inherited it from their parents, and on and on and back and back to the dawn of humanness, when hominids began turning the physical difference between male and female bodies into ways of defining and understanding what it means to be human.[1]

Like everyone else I know, I was born into a world that assumed that everyone was either male or female. I was identified as male from the "It's a boy" that proclaimed my birth, an announcement that, it was understood, described not only my genitalia but also my future. Before I even had a name, that "It's a boy" defined me as being fundamentally like my father and fundamentally different from my mother, as a future husband, father, grandfather, as one of the few who could pass on my family name, as someone who would be taught to live up to masculine standards of behavior, appearance, and achievement, and who, despite being covered in my mother's blood, was already draped in the invisible robes of male privilege and power.

Before I learned to read, before I knew that I was American or Jewish, before I could count to ten or color inside the lines, I, like most children, had already mastered the basic vocabulary of gender: "he" and "she," "boy" and "girl," "brother and sister," "father" and "mother." Gender was my mother tongue, a tongue that lectured me constantly, teaching me who I was and wasn't, what I should and shouldn't want, wear, play with, enjoy, feel, express, expect, aspire to, and fear, tirelessly telling me what I must and couldn't be.

Nothing about this was unusual, or specific to me as a transgender child. This is how gender raises us. Whatever else there may be in our lives, in the beginning, there is gender.

But unlike the other kids I knew, I didn't like what gender taught me. From the day I entered preschool and tried to play with girls who ran away because they saw me as a boy, I was painfully aware that I was not what gender said I was. I was a boy who longed to be a girl, or a boy who was meant to be a girl, or a girl hidden inside a boy, or a failed boy, or an invisible girl. I knew that none of those statements made any sense, but I had no other language through which I could understand who or what I was. Boy or girl, male or female: those terms were as fixed as "up" and "down," and, like up and down, they defined my limits and my longings. Gender, like another form of gravity, held me down, chaining me to a body that kept me from joining those who, it seemed to me, floated effortlessly through the sky of girl- and womanhood, those who were, really were, what gender told me I was not and could never be.

Now that I have watched two daughters grow up, I'm not sure how many of the girls I knew would have agreed that gender, to them, meant floating effortlessly. From conservative country singers to radical feminist scholars, the world is full of women bearing witness to the fact that the gravity of gender weighs everyone down, dragging us toward loves and lives that can drown our dreams, break our hearts, betray our hopes, and hold us back from becoming who we feel are or should have been.

But just as we rely on the gravity that keeps us from flying to ground us in the world, we rely on gender to ground ourselves and our friendships, families, and social relationships in a shared sense of what human beings are. Binary gender has never had a place for me, but I still rely on it to help me name and know those I love: I call my female parent "mother," my male child "son," my female child "daughter," my spouse "wife"; I recognize my closest friends as "women," and I want others to recognize me as "she." Even feminist thinkers who have devoted their lives to demonstrating the injuries and injustices of binary gender depend in their analyses on gender's power to divide humanity into males and females, men and women.[2]

In short, as hard as we may find it to live with binary gender, it seems to be harder to live without it, a situation that reminds me of a joke Woody

Allen tells at the end of *Annie Hall*: "Guy walks into a psychiatrist's office and says, 'Hey doc, my brother's crazy! He thinks he's a chicken.' Then the doc says, 'Why don't you turn him in?' Then the guy says, 'I would but we need the eggs.' I guess that's how I feel about relationships. They're totally crazy, irrational, and absurd, but we keep going through [them] because we need the eggs."[3]

Physical sex aside, most of our ideas about what it means to be a man or a woman are just that—ideas. However true they may seem to us, however passionately we may believe them, we know that other people in other places and times have held different ideas that seemed just as true to them. But like the guy in the joke, most of us, even scholars who study those ideas for a living, seem to need the eggs, the social and psychological benefits, we get from binary gender.

Many of those benefits come from the ways in which binary gender simplifies the messiness of humanity. No matter how different others' bodies, families, histories, religions, and cultures may be, the gender binary assures us that everyone is either male or female. No matter how our own bodies are altered by aging, accident, or illness, no matter how our circumstances, emotions, desires, or beliefs may change, no matter how complicated or conflicted our feelings may be, the gender binary assures that we are what we have always been: male or female, sons or daughters, men or women.

Given how much we rely on the gender binary to understand ourselves and others, it's not surprising that many people aren't sure what to do with folks like me, who don't fit binary definitions of male and female: which words to use when referring to us (common courtesy dictates using the pronouns we prefer, but things get more complicated when it comes to identifying us as mothers or fathers, sons or daughters, sisters or brothers, or even referring to past and present versions of us); where we belong when it comes to single-sex spaces like public restrooms, dormitories, prisons, men's and women's schools, competitive sports, homeless shelters, and so on; whether to see us as part of, or threats to, community and society. In most states, it is legal to deny us employment and housing; many religious communities consider it not only appropriate but also morally required to exclude us. Even among those who support equal protections and rights for transgender people, many wonder how accepting us might change the aspects of their lives that are based on binary gender. Some who oppose transgender acceptance even deny that we are who and what we say we are, arguing that transgender identities aren't identities at all, but sexual fetishes, psychological disorders, attention-getting stunts, "lifestyle choices," or affronts to God, morality, and the natural (binary) order on which, they believe, everything depends. Many traditional religious communities expel openly transgender members, oppose antidiscrimination laws, and consider transgender people to be mentally or spiritually ill.

Jews and Christians who object to accepting transgender people often point to the first chapter of Genesis, which declares that God created human beings male and female (Gen. 1:27), a verse that is frequently interpreted as meaning that binary gender is built into God's design for humanity. Because God created the first human beings male and female, anyone who claims to be something other than male or female is delusionally or sinfully perverting what God intends human beings to be. Such interpretations make it seem as though traditional religious communities cannot accept people who are not simply male or female without rejecting the Bible and the divine order of creation.

But even in ancient times, the rabbis of the Talmud recognized that reading this verse as a divine decree that human beings can only be male or female doesn't fit the facts of human physiology. They knew that while most human bodies fit binary norms, some are what we now call "intersex," and have characteristics that make it impossible to categorize them as male or female. For these rabbis, the questions raised by people who don't fit binary gender categories were not theological or moral, but practical: how can people who are neither male nor female fit into communities governed according to laws and traditions that assume everyone is either one or the other? Whatever we think of how the rabbis answered this question, their discussions make it clear that they believed that Jews who could not be categorized as male or female should be accepted both as members of Jewish communities who were bound by God's law and as human beings created in the image of God.[4]

But the rabbis were not discussing gender, the meanings and roles we base on physical differences between male and female bodies; they were discussing physical sex. It is one thing to recognize the existence of intersex people whose bodies don't fit binary categories. It is another to recognize transgender people, whose bodies do fit the categories of male and female but who do not identify with the sex of our bodies, or the gender roles we were assigned when our infant (or, these days, prenatal) maleness or femaleness was announced.

It is hard to find places in the Torah or the religious traditions that grew out of it that distinguish gender from physical sex the way transgender people do and the way communities must in order to understand and accept us. But the opening chapters of Genesis tell us that humanity was created before gender, and that the gender binary was created not by God, but by Adam. As we examine the genesis of gender, we find that the biblical account of the creation of humanity invites even traditionally religious readers to separate human ideas about binary gender from God's conception of what it means to be human.

The Birth of the Binary

Like many transgender people, I have spent my entire life on the lookout for signs of gender. To me, gender is everywhere in the human world, stamped on every face and figure, shouting from ads, singing pop songs, starring in every show.

But when I read the first chapter of Genesis, other than the gendered verbs and pronouns required by biblical Hebrew, gender isn't there. God creates light and dark, day and night, sky and earth, sun and moon, seas and stars, animals and plants, without referring to maleness or femaleness. That's why it's so striking when we are told that God created human beings "male and female": "And God said, 'Let us make [humanity] in our image, after our likeness. They shall rule the fish of the sea, the birds of the sky, the cattle, the whole earth, and all the creeping things that creep on earth.' So God created [humanity] in God's own image, in the image of God God created [them]; male and female God created them" (Gen. 1:26–27).[5] This is the first time Genesis distinguishes between male and female, and it seems to suggest that that division (a trait our species shares with many others) is a defining mark of humanity.

But there is no sign here or in the rest of this chapter that "male and female" carry the social, psychological, or other meanings we call "gender." Gender doesn't merely distinguish between male and female bodies; it gives this difference meaning, assigning different roles and characteristics to people with male and female bodies. At this point in creation, neither God nor the Torah treats males and females differently. Both are "created in the image of God," and in the verses that immediately follow, God blesses and instructs humanity without distinguishing one from another: "God blessed them, and God said to them, 'Be fertile and increase, fill the earth and master it; and rule the fish of the sea, the birds of the sky, and all the living things that creep on earth.' God said, 'See, I have given you every seed-bearing plant . . . and every tree that has seed-bearing fruit; they shall be yours for food'" (Gen. 1:28–29). Here, God addresses all human beings in the same terms, without distinguishing males from females: all humans are created in God's image, rule over other creatures, and are ordered to be vegetarians. As far as God is concerned—and God's perspective is the only one the text offers—differences in physical sex here have none of the meaning (assignment of different roles, characteristics, feelings, desires, earning capacity, authority, and so on, to males and females) that marks the presence of gender.

But by specifically mentioning that humanity is created male and female—by singling out that difference among all human physical variations—Genesis 1 lays the foundation for the gender binary. Actually, the first stone of the gender binary was laid at the beginning of creation, when God, distinguishing light from darkness, creates the first binary: "When God began to create heaven and earth—the earth being unformed and void, with darkness over the surface of the deep and a wind from God sweeping over the water—God said, 'Let there be light'; and there was light. God saw that the light was good, and God separated the light from the darkness. God called the light Day, and the darkness God called Night. And there was evening, and there was morning, a first day" (Gen. 1:1–5).

To most people, the idea that light and darkness are not only different from one another but are binary opposites that are mutually exclusive seems obvious: what's light isn't dark, and where darkness is present light is not. But according to the second verse of Genesis, darkness existed before light, and when, in verse 3, God says, "Let there be light," light is created as an independent entity, without regard to the darkness that preceded its creation. At this point, as rabbinic commentators noted, light and darkness have not yet become opposites, or even separate (because God hasn't yet separated them).[6] As a result, when God says that "the light was good," it doesn't imply that the darkness was bad, any more than it implies that "the deep" on which the darkness rested was bad. But when God separates light from darkness, light and darkness become binary categories. From here on, light and darkness are mutually exclusive: where there is light, there is no darkness, and vice versa.

Like the creation of human beings "male and female," the light/darkness binary refers to a purely physical distinction, without symbolic or other meanings. But as we see in verse 5, once physical reality is divided into categories, those categories tend to be associated with other binaries that *do* give them symbolic meanings. When "God called the light Day, and the darkness God called Night," God associates light/darkness with the day/night binary, turning a way of distinguishing degrees of illumination into a way of describing the human experience of time.

To most of us, it seems natural to associate light with day and darkness with night. But though day is usually lighter and night is usually darker, people who live near the poles often experience days of darkness and nights of light. Nonetheless, we still call those days "days" and those nights "nights." That's the power of binaries. They organize reality so effectively that they tend to seem like built-in features of existence rather than human interpretations of it.

Genesis 1 moves on after associating light and darkness with day and night, but most cultures pile on many more binary associations. For example, because light enables us to see, and seeing is associating with knowing, light is often associated with understanding and darkness with ignorance. Similarly, because being able to see makes us feel safe and being unable to see frightens us, light is often associated with goodness and darkness with evil. Associations like these expand the physical distinction between light and darkness into a complex web of symbols and metaphors.

But even the binary light/darkness interprets rather than describes reality. From a scientific perspective, "light" is a vague term that refers to the part of the electromagnetic spectrum visible to human eyes; "darkness" has no scientific meaning at all. The binary light/darkness reduces the complexity of reality into simple either/or terms that are easy to use and understand. If Genesis were written in the language of science, the statement "And God called the light Day, and the darkness God called Night" would read something like this: "And God called the period of time when the yet-uncreated human residents of the yet-uncreated planet not yet called 'Earth' would generally perceive the greatest amount of visible electromagnetic radiation 'Day,' and the period of time when they would generally perceive the least amount of visible electromagnetic radiation 'Night.'" If Genesis had avoided binaries in favor of precise physical descriptions, the Bible would never have become a best seller.

Binaries aren't accurate, but they are appealing. In fact, their inaccuracy is what makes them so appealing. They make it easy to organize and describe messy, complicated realities, and they even sound good, lending themselves to the kind of rhythmic, tick-tock parallelism that can make biblical proverbs and political rhetoric so effective: "You're either with us or against us," "There is right, and there is wrong," "The situation is black and white," and so on.

My favorite example of the power of binaries is the genre of jokes that begin, "There are two kinds of people in this world . . . ," which make fun of the way binaries—gender binary, I'm looking at you—claim to account for all of humanity in a few simple words. For example, "There are two kinds of people in this world: people who believe there are two kinds of people in this world, and people who don't." Most of us, including me, are both. We know there are as many kinds of people in this world as there are people—seven billion and counting—and we often rely on binary categories to quickly and easily describe them.

Gender and Loneliness

No binary is more powerful than the gender binary, which has been used to interpret everything from personal tastes to the structure of the universe, and has defined so many lives that Sigmund Freud famously said "Biology" (being born male or female) "is destiny."

As we saw above, the male/female binary introduced in Genesis 1 refers to physical sex, not gender, but it is not surprising that this, and only this, aspect of human bodies is mentioned. Binary gender—by which I mean any system that gives social or other meaning to the difference between male and female bodies—is a fundamental feature of every culture we know of.[7] I'm not suggesting that any particular version of binary gender is universal, hardwired into our brains and souls, or even stable. I have seen enormous changes in what people think it means to be a woman or a man over the course of my lifetime, and whenever I walk along a crowded street, I see many individual and cultural variations in how people express maleness and femaleness. But almost everywhere I look, I see people acting in ways that reflect the influence of binary gender.

Just as the light/darkness binary drastically oversimplifies the nature of electromagnetic radiation, so too every version of binary gender drastically oversimplifies the nature of humanity. As Joanne Meyerowitz describes in her history of transsexuality, even in the early twentieth century, scientists noted that

> [i]n its earliest stages the human embryo did not manifest its sex, and in its later development its sexual differentiation remained partial. The similarities of male and female reproductive organs seems to reveal their common origins: testis resembled ovary, and penis resembled clitoris. All males maintained vestiges of the female, and all females, vestiges of the male. Men had nipples and rudimentary breasts. The embryonic Müllerian duct, which developed into fallopian tubes, uterus, and vagina in woman, remained undeveloped in the man, and the Wolffian body and duct, which developed into the vas deferens, seminal vesicle, and epididymis in the man, remained undeveloped in the woman.[8]

In other words, even bodies that fit physical norms of maleness or femaleness don't fit the male/female binary, because the binary implies that when it comes to sex-related organs, male and female bodies are completely different. Like light and darkness before God separated them, physical maleness and femaleness are not mutually exclusive; all bodies include aspects of both.[9]

When we turn from physical sex to gender, the mismatch between the simplicity of the male/female binary categories and the complexity of human beings becomes even clearer. No matter what we believe it means to be male or female, few if any of us always and only fit those definitions. Even people who are not transgender feel or want things that binary gender categories tell us we shouldn't, and do things we are told we can't or shouldn't do.

But if binary gender categories fit humanity so badly, why do most people in most times and places insist on defining ourselves as male or female?

For me, the answer is simple: however poorly binary gender categories may fit me (and when I was living as a male I knew I wasn't, they fit me very poorly indeed), being seen as male or female is better than being alone. I grew up terrified that if those around me—my family, my teachers, my friends—knew that I wasn't really the boy they thought I was, they would shun me, exile me from home, school, and community. And I was right to be afraid. Even today, transgender kids make up a disproportionate share of homeless youth.

My fear of being alone was so great that for over forty years, I did daily violence to myself in order to fit the male identity I was assigned when the nurse who delivered me said, "It's a boy." It hurt to live as a man, but I knew that if I didn't, instead of being loved as a son, a husband, or a father, I would be seen as something monstrously, unlovably other. Maleness was a mask that hid who I knew myself to be, but it was a mask that enabled others to recognize me as human. Even the suicidal despair to which living as a man drove me seemed better than being alone.

The Torah doesn't talk about how it feels to be transgender, but it does speak to the longing to be known and loved that drove me to live so long as a man. In fact, according to the second chapter of Genesis, that is why gender was created: so human beings would not feel alone.

In chapter 1, humanity is created collectively, but in chapter 2, the creation of humanity begins with the creation of a single person, Adam: "[T]he LORD God formed man from the dust from the earth. [God] blew into his nostrils the breath of life, and the man became a living being" (Gen. 2:7). As in the first chapter, humanity here is created with sex (as the term "man" suggests, Adam is physically male), but not with gender. Gender is a system for giving meaning to the differences between male and female bodies, and at this point, there are no differences. Adam is the only one of his kind.

God gives Adam a home, a place to live—the Garden of Eden—and a purpose for living (taking care of the Garden [2:15]). God even gives him a law to keep—the famous prohibition against eating the fruit of the Tree of the Knowledge of Good and Evil. The man has a body, a soul, a home, work, food to eat, a relationship with God, and the beginning of morality, but he is not yet fully human, because though some of us enjoy living in solitude, as a species, human beings are social animals. As God reflects in verse 18, "It is not good for man to be alone."

And the man is very, very alone. In Genesis 1, humanity is created after all the other creatures, but in this chapter, Adam is created first—he's the only living thing on earth other than vegetation. In an effort to give him companionship, God "form[s] out of the earth all the wild beasts and all the birds of the sky" and parades them before Adam (2:19). Adam names the creatures, but, even though they, like him, were formed from the earth, he doesn't recognize any of them as the "fitting helper"—literally, "the helper who is his opposite"—he longs for (2:20). Finally, God gets it: Adam needs a creature whose body is akin to his own. That is why, instead of forming the woman from the earth, God forms her from Adam's body: so the man will see the woman as fundamentally like him, and no longer feel alone:

> So the LORD God cast a deep sleep upon the man, and he slept;
> and, while he slept, [God] took one of his ribs . . . And the LORD
> God fashioned the rib that [God] had taken from the man into a
> woman; and [God] brought her to the man. Then the man said,
> This one at last
> Is bone of my bones
> And flesh of my flesh.
> This one shall be called Woman,
> For from man was she taken.
> Hence a man leaves his father and mother and clings to his wife,
> so that they become one flesh. (Gen. 2:21–23)

As in Genesis 1:27, humanity here is created male and female, and as in the first chapter, in this story, the difference between male and female bodies is much less important than what human beings have in common. Those physical differences would surely have been striking to a man who had never seen a human body other than his own, but Adam ("the man") notices first the woman's physical kinship to him, the shared humanity he didn't find in other creatures: "This one at last is bone of my bones, and flesh of my flesh."

That recognition of common humanity inspires Adam to invent gender, that is, to interpret the differences between male and female bodies as implying different but intimately related identities: "This one shall be called Woman, for from man was she taken." This moment, when Adam begins to give human meaning to divinely created (but thus far not divinely interpreted) maleness and femaleness, represents the biblical genesis of gender, and the first budding of the gender binary.[10]

At this point, the gender binary is not concerned with sexual desire, reproduction, or male privilege; it is a means of naming the differences between the man and the woman in ways that emphasize their kinship. Of course, in Adam's (and Genesis's) male-centered account, it is the man who does the naming, and the woman who, according to Adam, is defined in relationship to man, "for from man was she taken."

But Adam's gender binary defines not only the woman; it also defines him. Before the woman was created, "man" was a unique term for a unique being. The binary man/woman demotes Adam from a supreme, species-defining individual to someone who is defined in relation to the woman, just as the woman is defined in relation to him.

Adam doesn't mind the demotion; in fact, he is delighted, because being defined by the gender binary means he is no longer alone. Even though he and the woman are the only human beings in the universe, Adam's invention of the gender binary leads immediately to a vision of a future filled with gender-based relationships that affirm that, despite their differences, men and women are, in the end, "one flesh": "Hence a man leaves his father and mother and clings to his wife, so that they become one flesh" (Gen. 2:24). In this vision, the gender binary is the root from which not just romantic relationships and family but also human history, imagined here as a series of conflicts between loyalty to parents and heterosexual attachments, grows. To express gender's rapidly expanding significance, the Torah adds two new binaries, "father/mother" and "husband/wife," to the original association of male/female and man/woman.[11]

Adam's enthusiastic response to the woman suggests many of the benefits we receive from binary gender. When we define ourselves as men and women rather than as unique individuals, we, like Adam, know we are not alone: the gender binary defines everyone with a male or female body as being like, essentially similar to, half the human race, and offers us a variety of roles (mother, father, husband, wife, son, daughter, boyfriend, girlfriend, and so on) that relate us to those in the other half.

But despite Adam's enthusiasm for the gender binary, there are already signs of trouble in paradise. As feminist critics have long pointed out, though humanity is created equally male and female in chapter 1, chapter 2 is all about the man: God forms Adam first, designs the Garden for him, creates the animals for his benefit, and invites him to name them. Only then, to relieve the man's isolation, does God create the woman. Though Adam and the woman presumably saw one another simultaneously, the story tells us only about Adam's response to seeing her, not her response to seeing him. (The woman, as they say, is seen and not heard.) In short, the creation of humanity is presented as a story about a man, his needs, and a woman who is literally created to fulfill them—a bias that the Torah presents as continuing into the future it describes as consisting of men leaving their parents for their wives.

But even though Adam and the Torah present it from a male perspective, gender here is a means of defining personal and family relationships, not a patriarchal system that is based on male dominance or female submission. As Phyllis Trible points out, in chapter 2, neither God nor Adam says anything that identifies the gender binary with male dominance or female submission;[12] even Adam's male-centered vision of a gendered future, which focuses on the drama of men leaving their parents for their wives, ends on an egalitarian note, with husband and wife becoming "one flesh."

But whatever its virtues may have been, this Edenic vision of gender is lost, along with Eden itself, in chapter 3, when God responds to the eating the fruit of the Tree of the Knowledge of Good and Evil by cursing the man and the woman in terms that transform binary gender into an engine of inequality:

And to the woman [God] said,

"I will make most severe

Your pangs in childbearing;

In pain shall you bear children.

Yet your urge shall be for your husband,

And he shall rule over you."

To Adam [God] said, "Because you did as your wife said and ate

of the tree about which I commanded you, 'You shall not eat of it,'

Cursed be the ground because of you;

By toil shall you eat of it

All the days of your life. . . .

By the sweat of your brow

Shall you get bread to eat. (Gen. 3:16–17)

God's punishments magnify the consequences of being male and being female, decreeing that the woman is to be ruled by the man and burdened by childbirth, while the man is to toil for food. These curses transform binary gender from a means of establishing intimate relationships into a system of oppression, in which social roles, privilege, and power are unequally divided on the basis of maleness and femaleness.

Even here, at the mythic dawn of patriarchy, Genesis hints that there could and should be a better form of gender. God presents patriarchy as a curse on men as well as women.[13] And though patriarchy is the final step in the biblical genesis of gender, it is presented not as an inevitable outgrowth of inherent differences between males and females but as the unforeseen, tragic consequence of human violation of God's command—in Christian terms, of original sin. Had the woman and the man not eaten the fruit, the story implies, gender would never have become patriarchal.

But these are hints of a paradise that certainly was lost. Although the gender binary has taken innumerable forms, most fulfill the biblical curse of patriarchy all too well. And while it is generally better to rule than to be ruled over, as the biblical curse suggests, men as well as women suffer from patriarchal forms of the gender binary that turn biology, the physical difference between male and female bodies, into social destiny. From this perspective, the patriarchal form of gender we see in most of the Torah, in which women are defined primarily as mothers and are ruled over by men who are responsible for providing food for the family, is not a sign of God's original intentions for humanity but a curse humanity continues to endure.

Genesis and Transgender Identities

Religious traditionalists often point to the version of gender we see in the Garden of Eden as representing God's idea of what human beings are and should be. That's the assumption behind statements like "God made Adam and Eve, not Adam and Steve," which suggests that because Adam and Eve were heterosexual, all people should be heterosexual. But the version of the gender binary we see in the opening chapters of Genesis doesn't only leave out gay people; it leaves out most kinds of people. This is a gender binary built for two. Adam and Eve seem to have been created as adults and they have not yet had children, so there are no sisters or brothers, best male or female friends, grandmothers or grandfathers, or, for that matter, girls or boys. Clearly, this version of the gender binary is not meant to define all, or even most, of humanity.

In most of the Torah, as in our lives today, gender is a complicated system that shapes family life, social roles, laws and rituals, politics, morality (men and women are judged by different standards), and even the ways in which the Torah describes God. But the version of gender we see at the end of the third chapter of Genesis is still quite simple. Because there are only two human beings in the world, maleness and femaleness don't yet have symbolic significance. When God curses Adam and Eve, the curses represent practical punishments for their actions, not statements about the moral or spiritual qualities of males and females. At this point, gender serves only three purposes: it ensures that, despite their differences, male and female bodies are recognized as akin to one another, bone of the same bone, flesh of one human flesh; it fosters family connections by giving males and females roles (mother/father, husband/wife) that relate them to one another; and, in the curses, it assigns males and females different levels of authority and different kinds of work.

But even in this simple form, the gender binary we see at the end of chapter 3 is still a binary. It assumes that all human beings will be either and always male or female, men or women. Mothers will never be fathers, husbands will never become wives. There is no room in this or any version of the gender binary for people like me, people who are not simply male or female, people for whom gender is not defined by physical sex.

Although the version of gender that emerges by the end of the first three chapters of Genesis does not speak to people who don't fit binary categories, the story of the genesis of gender does. Adam is human before he is gendered; his humanity does not depend on him fitting into a binary gender system, on being a man as opposed to a woman. The Torah presents gender not as a built-in aspect of humanity decreed by God, but as a human creation, born out of Adam's response to Eve. As new and startling as transgender identities can seem, in this regard they are direct descendants of the biblical genesis of gender: like Adam's woman/man binary, transgender identities are human inventions, attempts to understand and express who we are in relation to others, so that we will not feel alone.

But Adam invents gender as a way of recognizing that the woman and man, despite their physical differences, are kin to one another. To be openly transgender means being seen as someone whose differences can't be understood in terms of binary gender—and, all too often, that means not being seen as "bone of my bone, and flesh of my flesh," but as incomprehensibly other. Some transgender people enjoy being what gender theorist Kate Bornstein calls "gender outlaws"; some of us find friends and family, partners and communities, who love us despite, or because of, our otherness.[14] However, for too many of us, being seen as transgender means exile from family and community, loss of housing and employment, verbal and physical abuse, isolation, and, too often, suicide or murder.

As a culture, we are still working to develop an understanding of what it means to be transgender, of how transgender identities relate us to as well as distinguish us from people who fit into binary gender categories. The increasing visibility of transgender people means that, like it or not, we are all engaged in the process of figuring out how recognizing that some people are not simply male or female changes our understanding of gender. I spent most of my life in hiding, but now transgender people run for public office, are interviewed on news programs, publish books and essays, appear on TV shows and in movies, and are subjects of political speeches and Supreme Court cases. Many religious denominations now have openly transgender clergy, and some have developed prayers and rituals specifically for transgender people. More and more institutions and facilities include restrooms, policies, and accommodations designed with transgender people in mind. Even in communities that don't accept transgender identities as valid, transgender people are discussed and debated. And though it may be decades before such debates are settled, the widespread recognition that there are people who are not simply male or female is slowly, spottily, but profoundly transforming our understanding of gender, and thus of what it means to be human.

The ideas that gender is a human invention and that gender can change may seem startlingly new, but they are there in the opening chapters of Genesis. Adam's version of gender consists of a single binary, man and woman. But in the verse that follows his response to first seeing Eve, gender is transformed, as the Torah expands the gender binary to include the mothers and fathers, wives and husbands, who will populate the future. When God curses Adam and Eve, gender once more changes before our eyes. The Torah does not envision transgender identities, but the idea that gender can not just change but change radically, in a single generation, is at the heart of the biblical genesis of gender.

Above all, Genesis lays the ground for accepting people who don't fit binary gender categories by reminding us that people don't have to be gendered to be human. As we saw, when God creates human beings at the end of Genesis 1, they are created without gender, because the differences between male and female bodies have not yet been given meaning; in the second creation story in Genesis 2, humanity is again created without gender, because God at first only created Adam, who, because he is unique, cannot have a gender.

By showing us that we do not need gender to be human, the Torah not only offers a basis for acceptance of the humanity of transgender people. It also frees us to recognize the ways in which non-transgender people do not fit binary gender categories, to notice that there are women who have facial hair and men who don't, women without breast tissue and men with plenty, women who are over six feet tall and men who are under five feet, women who don't have uteruses and men who don't have testicles, women with low voices and men with high voices. When we remember that, as the first two chapters of Genesis show, our humanity does not depend on gender, we can acknowledge, without fear or shame, the aspects of ourselves that don't fit the gender to which we have been assigned, and the ways in which thinking of ourselves as only and always male or female limits our understanding of who we are and what we can be. In this sense, the biblical account of the genesis of gender lays the ground for accepting the dazzling variety not just of transgender people, but of humanity.

In the Image of God, God Created Them

But what about the Torah's declaration that God created human beings "male and female"? Even if we agree that "male and female" refers to physical sex rather than gender, doesn't this verse show that the division of humanity into males and females is an immutable, God-given feature of humanity, an essential aspect of God's design?

Let's take a closer look at Genesis 1:26–27. Here, for the first time in the unfolding of creation, the Torah reports not only God's reality-shaping words but also God's intentions: "And God said, 'Let us make [humanity] in our image, after our likeness. They shall rule the fish of the sea, the birds of the sky, the cattle, the whole earth, and all the creeping things that creep on earth.' And God created [humanity] in God's own image, in the image of God [God] created [them]; male and female God created them" (Gen. 1:26–27).

According to verse 26, God has two intentions in creating humanity: human beings are designed to reflect the image of God, an idea repeated twice in the verse and twice in the next, and to rule over everything else on earth.[15] In the verse, God is not concerned about creating humanity male and female. Although verse 27 tells us that God did so, that is mentioned only once, in passing, and, as we have seen, the blessings and instructions God gives the newly created human beings do not distinguish between males and females. Maleness and femaleness matter a great deal to human beings, but the first chapter of Genesis portrays them as mattering very little to God, whose design for humanity focuses not on details of anatomy but on humanity's connection to God and relation to other living things.

Genesis-based arguments against transgender identities tend to assume that the statement that God created human beings in God's image is directly connected with the division of humanity into male and female. According to this view, people like me who refuse to fit ourselves into binary gender categories are rejecting our relationship with God. To affirm that relationship, we must accept that we are either and only male or female, and live in ways that express, through the conventions of gender, the maleness or femaleness of the bodies God gave us.

But the Torah doesn't tell us what being created in the image of God means, or explain how human beings are similar to the invisible, disembodied, time- and space-transcending Creator of the Universe. That, to me, is the point of reading God and the Torah from a transgender perspective: to better understand the kinship between humanity and the inhuman, bodiless God in whose image we are created, a God who does not fit any of the categories through which human beings define ourselves and one another. From the time I first read Genesis as a child who knew that I didn't fit the male/female binary, it has been clear to me that the "image of God" has nothing to do with sex, gender, human differences, or human bodies. Whatever the benefits of gender as a means of fostering human relationships, if our goal is to recognize our kinship with God, then we need to look to the aspects of humanity that can't be conceived in terms of gender, to the ways in which we, like the God in whose image we are created, exceed or confound human categories.

We don't have to identify as transgender to engage in this effort. As I said above, none of us exactly fits human categories, and all of us can and should try to look past sex and gender, bodies and binaries, to understand what in humanity reflects the image of God. But being transgender forces me and many transgender people to recognize the ways we don't fit human categories, because the aspects of ourselves that don't make sense in terms of binary gender are at the heart of our sense of who we are. Like God, we are used to being present and either invisible or seen as incomprehensible and sometimes terrifying. We are accustomed to living in the wilderness, beyond the bounds of binaries and the world that is based upon them. It can be lonely there, and hard, but according to the Torah, as we will see in the next chapter, it is often in the wilderness that human beings come closest to God.

TWO

TRANS EXPERIENCE IN THE TORAH

"Who are You, My Son?":
Recognizing Trans Experience in the Torah

Most of the encounters between God and human beings we see in the Torah take place in the wilderness—in sparsely inhabited places where nomadic shepherds such as Abraham, Isaac, Jacob, and Moses graze their flocks, or in the desert where the Israelites wander for decades before entering the Promised Land.[1] But for much of my life, I took it for granted that none of those encounters takes place in the kind of wilderness I referred to at the end of chapter 1, the wilderness beyond gender roles and categories that transgender people know so well.

I was wrong. The Torah doesn't portray transgender people—it doesn't describe anyone as being other than male or female, or as moving, as I have moved, from one side of the gender binary to the other. But the Torah does show Abraham, Sarah, and Jacob abandoning or violating their assigned gender roles (the gender roles they are expected to perform), and it associates these experiences, which I call "trans experiences," with their relationships to God.

Few people identify as transgender, but most people have trans experiences: experiences, however brief, of acting in ways that don't fit our usual gender roles. Unlike transgender identities, most trans experiences don't disrupt or challenge the gender binary distinction between male and female. People continue to be seen, and to see themselves, as male or female before, during, and after trans experiences that displace us from our assigned gender roles; we remain men or women, even if we feel like, or become, different *kinds* of men and women.

For many of us, our most intense trans experiences occur during adolescence, a time when we seem to be neither and both the boys or girls we were and the men or women we are growing into, a time when our bodies, our sense of who we are, and our manner of presenting ourselves, keep changing in ways that often baffle those around us.[2]

We find the clearest examples of trans experience in the Torah in the story of Jacob, who impersonates his older brother Esau to steal his first-born blessing. Jacob and Esau are both male and are born almost simultaneously, but they are assigned at birth to very different gender roles. Because Esau emerges from the womb first, he is considered the firstborn, heir not only to Isaac's worldly possessions but also to the relationship with God that Isaac inherited from his father, Abraham. Though Jacob is born holding onto his brother's heel, he is considered the second-born, expected to accept the authority of his older brother, who, after their father's death, will become the head of the family. Like the gender binary, this law of inheritance, called "primogeniture," creates a lifelong, life-determining binary division between males who are and those who aren't firstborn sons.[3] And like the gender binary, primogeniture turns biology, in this case birth order, into destiny. The way male children are raised, the roles they are assigned, and the futures toward which they are steered are determined by whether they are or aren't firstborn sons.

Before Jacob dresses up as his brother, the Torah describes them not only as different kinds of men (firstborn and second-born) but also as binary opposites: Jacob is smooth, Esau is hairy; Jacob is domestic, Esau is a hunter; Jacob is close to his mother, Esau to his father. Though they are both male and both men, Jacob is portrayed as feminine, at least compared to the hypermasculine Esau. They live different kinds of lives, wear different kinds of clothes, do different work, bond with different parents. Just as the differences the gender binary attributes to men and women have little to do with physical sex, none of these differences between Jacob and Esau has anything to do with inheritance or birth order. Even so, the Torah presents them as though they were natural consequences of the gender roles they were assigned at birth, as unchangeable as the order in which they were born.

But even before Esau and Jacob are born, God tells their mother Rebekah that they will not ultimately be defined by the roles they are assigned at birth: "Two nations are in your womb . . . and the older shall serve the younger" (Gen. 25:23). Although we are not told whether Rebekah shares this prophecy with Jacob, our one glimpse of the brothers' early relationship suggests that Jacob was thinking along similar lines. Even as Jacob cooks and feeds his brother—actions that seem to acknowledge Esau's dominance—Jacob undermines Esau's firstborn status by insisting that Esau sell his birthright (the double share of inherited wealth to which he was entitled as firstborn) in exchange for Jacob's stew (Gen. 25:30–34).

Jacob's outrageous demand, made on the spur of the moment, suggests that he was waiting for a chance to seize Esau's birthright, that Jacob had for some time (perhaps all his life) had the trans experience of seeing himself in ways that did not fit the gender role he was assigned at birth. When he demands the birthright from Esau, Jacob engages in a different form of trans experience: the experience of expressing his inward rejection of the role he was born into by revealing to his brother that he is not content to be a second-born son. And after he acquires Esau's birthright, Jacob embarks on yet another kind of trans experience: by changing his inheritance status, he becomes a new kind of male, one who doesn't fit the firstborn/second-born binary: a male with the body of a second-born son but the birthright of a firstborn.

But acquiring the birthright doesn't seem to have changed Jacob's role within his family. He may feel more like a firstborn son, but he is still treated as a second-born, as we see when, years later, their father Isaac, now elderly and blind, declares that he wants to give Esau his "innermost blessing before I die" (Gen. 27:4). From the Torah's perspective, Isaac's blessing is the most important part of Isaac's legacy, for with it, Isaac passes on the relationship with God that he inherited from his father, Abraham. Isaac himself inherited that blessing as a second-born son after his older brother Ishmael was banished.[4] But despite that history, or maybe because of it, Isaac is determined to pass his blessing on to Esau, who is not only entitled to the blessing as Isaac's firstborn, but who is also his favorite son.

If God were committed to the gender binary idea that people are unchangeably defined by the gender roles we are assigned at birth, then either Esau would have been destined to inherit Isaac's relationship with God, or

Jacob would have been born first. But as God reveals to Rebekah before the twins are born, God intends for the younger brother to usurp the elder, prenatally linking God's blessing to trans experience.

Whether because of God's prophecy or her own preference, when Rebekah hears that Isaac is about to give Esau his blessing, she translates God's prophecy into practical action, working to help her younger son convince her blind husband that Jacob is his older brother to ensure that Jacob receives Isaac's blessing: "Rebekah then took the best clothes of her older son Esau . . . and had her younger son Jacob put them on; and she covered his hands and the hairless part of his neck with the skins of the kids" (Gen. 27:15–16).

Rebekah helps Jacob pass not only as a different man—Esau, whose clothes will give Jacob his older brother's distinctive smell—but also as a different kind of man, a man who will seem to Isaac's touch to embody Esau's masculinity.

Just as I and many transsexuals have felt, Jacob fears that his body will betray his gender presentation.[5] He tells his mother, "[M]y brother Esau is a hairy man, and I am smooth-skinned. If my father touches me, I shall seem to him as a trickster and bring upon myself a curse, not a blessing" (Gen. 27:11–12). Jacob fears that no matter how he presents himself, his father will recognize him for what he is: a "trickster" who is deceptively using signs of masculinity to prevent his father from identifying him with the body and gender role he was born to. Transsexuals are often seen by others as tricksters; in fact, my gender therapist gave me a letter to carry assuring police and other authorities that I was not presenting myself as a woman in order to commit fraud. But transsexuals present ourselves as the opposite of the gender we were assigned at birth to reveal, not to conceal, who we truly are. Jacob really *is* committing fraud, trying to pass as someone he knows he isn't to steal a blessing that isn't intended for him.[6]

Even though I knew that Jacob was not a transsexual when I read this story as a child, I saw it as a story about one of the most painful aspects of my own experience.[7] Jacob and I were both pretending to be sons we knew we weren't, hoping our parents wouldn't recognize the truth hidden beneath our clothes and skins. Like Jacob's, my life depended on clothing myself in a phony masculinity in order to receive my family's blessings of food, shelter, clothing, and love; and, like Jacob, I was terrified of the "curse" I was certain would come if my deception was discovered.

When Jacob purchases Esau's birthright, it seems that only he and his brother are aware of how Jacob's position has changed. But when Jacob steals the blessing, he not only temporarily passes as his firstborn brother; he publicly, permanently, transforms his gender role, ensuring that everyone, even his father, recognizes that he is no longer the man he was born to be. Although he is still Isaac's second-born, subject to the authority of his older brother, he is now endowed with a firstborn's material and spiritual inheritance. In this sense, perhaps we *can* read Jacob as a transgender person, someone who must abandon the gender roles he was assigned at birth in order to become the person who, as God's prophecy to Rebekah tells us, he was created to be.

The Torah doesn't tell us how Jacob felt while he was presenting himself as a man he knew wasn't, but it forces us to stand beside him in his father's tent, witnessing both his lies and Isaac's failure to recognize his own son:

[Jacob] went to his father and said, "Father." And [Isaac] said, "Yes, which of my sons are you?" Jacob said to his father, "I am Esau, your firstborn. . . . [E]at of my game, that you may give me your innermost blessing." Isaac said to his son, "How did you succeed so quickly, my son?" And he said, "Because the LORD your God granted me good fortune." Isaac said to Jacob, "Come closer that I may feel you, my son—[to determine] whether you are really my son Esau or not." So Jacob drew close to his father Isaac, who felt him and wondered. "The voice is the voice of Jacob, yet the hands are the hands of Esau." He did not recognize [Jacob], because his hands were hairy, like his brother Esau's hands; and so he blessed him. [Isaac] asked, "Are you really my son Esau?" And [after] he said, "I am," . . . his father Isaac said to him, "Come close and kiss me, my son"; and he went up and kissed him. And he smelled his clothes and he blessed him, saying, "Ah, the smell of my son is like the smell of the fields that the LORD has blessed." (Gen. 27:18–27)

I still feel sick when I watch Jacob assure his blind father that he really is the son his father thinks he is. My heart breaks when Isaac says, "Come close and kiss me, my son" and Jacob kisses him, even though his father believes his kiss is Esau's (Gen. 27:26). When Isaac, inhaling the smell of Esau's clothes, exclaims, "Ah, the smell of my son is like the smell of the fields the LORD has blessed," I feel the shame that Jacob does not seem to feel as he accepts the blessing inspired by his brother's scent, a blessing expressing his father's love for a man Jacob knows he isn't.

But this scene is not only about Jacob's deception of his father; it is also about Isaac's failure to recognize his son. Being misrecognized by those we are closest to—being identified not as who we are, but as who our family members wish we were—is a form of trans experience that is excruciatingly familiar to many transgender people. As we saw in chapter 1, Adam first invents binary gender to recognize and name his kinship with Eve. The version of gender I grew up with was much more sophisticated than Adam's, but it served the same function, enabling my family members to recognize and name who we were to one another: husband or wife, father or mother, daughter or son, sister or brother. Those names worked well to identify most of us. But in my case, as in Isaac's mistaking of Jacob for Esau, gender prevented my parents from recognizing who the child standing before them really was.

Unlike me, Jacob is lucky that his father relies on gender to identify his children. If he hadn't, Jacob's deception would probably have failed. From the moment Jacob enters his tent, Isaac doubts that the son sitting before him is the son he was expecting, asking, "Which of my sons are you?" When Isaac wonders how Esau could have found, killed, skinned, butchered, and cooked game so quickly, Jacob's pious response that "the LORD your God granted me good fortune" heightens Isaac's doubts, prompting him to seek physical proof that Jacob is Esau: "Come near," he tells his son, "that I may feel you" (Gen. 27:20–21). If he had touched Jacob's face, he would presumably have recognized his younger son's facial features. But instead, Isaac relies on gender to identify his son, touching his hands in search of the physical sign (hairiness) of the masculinity he associates with Esau.[8] As it did in my family's understanding of me, gender leads Isaac astray: "He did not recognize [Jacob], because his hands were hairy, like his brother Esau's hands; and so he blessed him" (Gen. 27:23).

But even after touching Jacob's goat-skin-covered hands, Isaac knows that something is wrong: "The voice is the voice of Jacob," he says, "yet the hands are the hands of Esau" (Gen. 27:22). The combination of Jacob's way of talking with Esau's hairiness gives Isaac a fleeting taste of a form of trans experience we now call "gender dysphoria": the sometimes extreme discomfort people feel when we cannot make sense of ourselves or others in terms of gender.[9]

I experienced gender dysphoria for most of my life, because binary gender categories gave me no way to reconcile my sense of being female with my male body and life. The mismatch between how I looked and who I was felt so extreme that even as a child, I was shocked to see a boy looking back at me from the mirror. Once I began living as myself, I saw that other people would sometimes experience gender dysphoria when they could not reconcile my presentation of myself as a woman with their experience of me as a man. That is the kind of gender dysphoria Isaac seems to feel in this scene: he knows from his son's voice and way of speaking that it must be Jacob standing before him, but the hairiness of his hands tells him it must be Esau, and he cannot make sense of the contradiction. Some people resolve the gender dysphoria they feel when they see me by deciding that because I was born male, I must be a man, no matter how I identify, look, or live. Isaac resolves his gender dysphoria in a similar way, deciding that the physical signs of gender are telling him who his son truly is.[10] When he does so, the Torah portrays gender not as a system of recognition, as it is for Adam when he recognizes Eve as "bone of my bone, flesh of my flesh," but as a system of misrecognition that can blind us even to the people we are closest to.

But the misrecognition in this scene represents more than Isaac's personal failure, and more, even, than the danger of relying on the external signs of gender to identify other people: it represents the triumph of God's will over human gender. Ever since Esau emerged from Rebekah's womb, Isaac has been waiting to give him this blessing; ever since he was old enough to know what being firstborn meant, Esau has waited to receive it. God's will, announced to Rebekah before the twins were born, demands that Esau be cheated out of the blessings that primogeniture has promised him, and that Jacob embrace the trans experience of presenting himself as a kind of man he isn't in order to become the person God meant him to be:

the younger who would rule the older, the third of the founding fathers of the Jewish people, the one who gives the name he later acquires, Israel, to the people who descend from him. No matter how strongly we sympathize with Isaac's and Esau's betrayal and disappointment, disapprove of Jacob's fraud, or believe that when it comes to gender, biology is and should be destiny, if we identify ourselves with any of the religions and cultures that grew out of the Torah, then we have to root for Jacob to succeed in impersonating his brother and becoming the kind of man he was not born to be.

"Leave Your Father's House": Trans Experience and the Covenant

The Torah portrays Jacob's trans experience as necessary for him to enter into the relationship with God that will later blossom into Judaism and the many religious traditions that have grown out of it. But Jacob's impersonation of Esau is not the first time the Torah directly links trans experience to relationship with God. The blessing Jacob steals was first given to his grandfather, Abraham (then called Abram), on the condition that Abraham abandon the firstborn role he was assigned at birth and follow God into the wilderness:

> The LORD said to Abram, "Go forth from your native land and
> from your father's house to the land that I will show you.
> I will make of you a great nation,
> And I will bless you,
> And you shall be a blessing.
> I will bless those who bless you
> And curse him that curses you;
> And all the families of the earth
> Shall bless themselves by you." (Gen. 12:1–3)

God's first words to Abraham—the foundation of the relationship with God that Jacob inherits—command him to turn his back on his firstborn role (and his 145-year-old father) in return for divine blessing. When God gives him this command, Abraham is seventy-five years old and has lived his whole life in his father's house. Although some rabbinic stories portray

Abraham as a born iconoclast who even as a child challenges his father's polytheistic beliefs, the Torah doesn't.[11] According to the Torah, before God speaks to him, Abraham has faithfully fulfilled his firstborn role by following his father, Terah, from their native city, Ur of the Chaldeans, to the city of Haran (Gen. 11:31). (Abraham's second-born brother, Nahor, stays behind.) Terah says that their goal is to reach Canaan, but when instead he settles in Haran, Abraham, his faithful firstborn heir, stays with him.

But when God tells him to go forth from the elderly Terah's house, Abraham, like his grandson Jacob many years later, does not hesitate to betray his father and violate the gender role he was born to. Without warning, apology, or farewell, Abraham abandons his father, taking with him his wife, Sarah (then called Sarai), and his nephew Lot, the only other relatives who accompanied Terah to Haran (Gen. 12:4–5). Jacob's betrayal of his father is more dramatic, but Abraham's is more devastating. Abraham not only violates his firstborn obligation to care for his father, who, the Torah tells us, will live for another sixty years after Abraham leaves him alone in a strange land. He also leaves his father impoverished, taking with him "all the wealth that they had amassed, and the persons that they had acquired in Haran" (12:5).

Like Jacob's, Abraham's trans experience—the experience of rejecting his assigned gender role—is presented by the Torah as both fulfillment of God's will and as required in order to receive God's blessing. And like Jacob, Abraham is transformed by his trans experience into a new kind of man, one who doesn't make sense in terms of primogeniture. On the one hand, Abraham becomes a firstborn who acts like a second-born by leaving his father's house rather than remaining as his support and heir; on the other hand, Abraham becomes a patriarch whose inheritance (God's promised blessings) and status come not from his father but from God.

I didn't identify with Abraham when I was a child. It wasn't until I was in the midst of my own family-shattering gender transition that I recognized Abraham's decision to leave his father's house as a form of trans experience and Abraham as a kindred spirit, someone who also overturns his life and family by leaving the gender roles he was born into. In Hebrew, God's first words to Abraham are *lekh lekha*, literally "Go to [or for] yourself" (Gen. 12:1). These words frame Abraham leaving his father's house not as a spiritual quest (God doesn't say *lech li*, "Go to [or for] Me") but as a self-centered act of becoming. That was also the way I understood my gender transition: like Abraham, I was going to myself, becoming a kind of person the gender system I was born into could not imagine. Unlike Abraham, who abandons and impoverishes his father, I continued to care for my family after I stopped living as the man I was supposed to be. But like Abraham, I had to leave my home in order to become myself, and like him, I did not know what life I would find in the wilderness beyond my assigned gender role.

For both Abraham and me, becoming ourselves involved changing our bodies, though unlike mine, Abraham's physical transformation was accomplished through flint knives, and was inflicted on every male in his household:

> When Abram was ninety years old and nine, the LORD appeared to Abram, and said to him, "I am El Shaddai. Walk in My ways and be blameless. . . . And you shall no longer be called Abram, but your name shall be Abraham, for I make you the father of a multitude of nations." . . . God further said to Abraham, "As for you, you and your offspring to come throughout the ages shall keep My covenant. Such shall be the covenant between Me and you and your offspring to follow which you shall keep: every male among you shall be circumcised. You shall circumcise the flesh of your foreskin, and that shall be the sign of the covenant between Me and you. And throughout the generations, every male among you shall be circumcised at the age of eight days." (Gen. 17:1–12)

By the time I was circumcised (on the eighth day after my birth, as God commands here), Jews had long accepted circumcision as a way of confirming rather than unsettling Jewish masculinity. But when Abraham circumcises the males in his household, there is no such thing as "Jewish masculinity," because there are no Jewish men. There is only Abraham, who physically expresses his relationship with God by surgically altering what even today is sometimes referred to as his "manhood."

Abraham's manhood-altering circumcision marks a new stage in the gender transition that began with his abandonment of his role as firstborn son. Aside from abandoning his father and his firstborn role, before his circumcision, Abraham was a familiar kind of Iron Age man: a husband, a father (to Ishmael), the patriarch of his small, wandering clan. Circumcision transforms him from the head of a single nomadic household into "the father of a multitude of nations," a transformation God marks by changing his name from "Abram" to "Abraham" (Gen. 17:5). Abraham's abandonment of his firstborn role was a private, family matter. His name change publicly signifies that he has become a different kind of man, a kind of man who had never before existed, one for which even the Torah doesn't provide a name: a Jewish man, a man whose circumcised body attests to his covenant with God.[12]

In the millennia since Abram became Abraham, circumcision has gone from being a masculinity-altering form of trans experience to a widespread gender norm among Jews and Muslims. But the practice of circumcision still symbolically echoes the link between trans experience and relationship with God, reminding us that what we call the Abrahamic religions began with Abraham's willingness to leave behind the gender role he had been assigned at birth and follow God into the wilderness beyond it.

"God Has Brought Me Laughter":
Feeling Trans Experience

In the stories of Abraham leaving his father's house and of Jacob impersonating his brother, the Torah portrays trans experience from the outside. We see Abraham and Jacob abandon the gender roles they were born to, but we don't know how they felt about themselves or their lives before, during, or after their trans experiences. We are not told whether they found the gender roles they were born into oppressive, or if they felt happier, more authentic, or more alive after they left those roles behind. Nor does the Torah tell us how they felt about the effects of their gender-altering actions on those around them. Did Abraham worry about the elderly father he abandoned or the wife he uprooted? Did Jacob feel guilt or shame toward the father he fleeced or the brother whose identity, blessing, and future he stole? The Torah does not say. Abraham and Jacob violate the gender roles they were born to without warning or apology, as though, once they have secured God's blessing, they don't care how others are affected by the ways they have changed themselves and their lives.

That is how gender transition often looks to non-transgender people: like a heartless, selfish decision to sacrifice our families to our own pursuit of blessing. The Torah makes it clear that Abraham and Jacob leave their assigned gender roles because God wants them to. From that perspective, feelings are irrelevant to their trans experiences. But when I try to explain why I stopped living as the man my family loved and started living as myself, all I can point to is feelings: my feelings that life as a man was a living death, and that only by expressing my female gender identity could I be authentic and truly alive. In fact, before I began the transition process, feelings made up most of my trans experience: the feeling that I was somehow really female; the feeling that my body was not mine; the feeling that I, like Jacob, was impersonating a male I wasn't, and that anyone who saw me as male (which is to say, everyone other than God) wasn't seeing me at all. My gender transition looked like a sudden, inexplicable decision to others, but to me, it was a desperate, last-ditch attempt to finally become the person I felt God created me to be.

In the story of Sarah's miraculous conception of Isaac after lifelong infertility, the Torah offers glimpses of the emotional aspects of trans experience. The Torah tells us that though Sarah is what her culture considers a successful woman in terms of being married and beautiful (even when she is sixty-five, Abraham fears that he may be killed by men who desire her [Gen. 12:11–13]), because Sarah cannot bear children and give her husband a male heir, her marriage is shadowed by her awareness that she is failing to be the woman she is supposed to be. In Genesis 16, Sarah's feeling of gender failure leads her to invite her husband to have sex with her servant Hagar, in hopes that Hagar will bear a son who Sarah (then called Sarai) can adopt as her own:

> And Sarai said to Abram, "Look, the LORD has kept me from
> bearing. Consort with my maid; perhaps I shall have a son [liter-
> ally, 'be built up'] through her." And Abram heeded Sarai's request.
> So Sarai, Abram's wife, took her maid, Hagar the Egyptian . . . and
> gave her to her husband Abram as a concubine. He cohabited with

Hagar and she conceived; and when she saw that she had conceived, her mistress was lowered in her esteem. And Sarai said to Abram, "The wrong done me is your fault! I myself put my maid in your bosom; now that she sees that she is pregnant, I am lowered in her esteem." . . . Abram said to Sarai, "Your maid is in your hands. Deal with her as you think right." Then Sarai treated her harshly, and she ran away from her. (Gen. 16:2–6)

Sarah presents her proposal that her husband have sex with her maid matter-of-factly, but it is clear that her feelings of failure have reached a crisis point. After a lifetime of infertility, only now, when she is in her eighties, does Sarah feel bad enough to engage in what seems to have been the common practice of forcing female servants to bear surrogate children.[13] Sarah's description of God as preventing her from bearing makes it clear that she has long tried and failed to have children. When she expresses hope that she may be "built up" through Hagar's fertility, we know that she feels she needs to be built up, that she feels she cannot build herself up, that she feels she has to have a son in order to become (be built up into) the woman she is supposed to be.

Hagar's immediate success in getting pregnant intensifies Sarah's feelings of gender failure. Rather than feeling built up, Sarah feels looked down upon by Hagar and presumably by her husband, whom she blames for going along with her proposal that he have a child with Hagar ("The wrong done me is your fault!" [Gen. 16:5]). With her husband's encouragement, Sarah takes her feelings out on Hagar, treating her so badly that the pregnant woman flees into the wilderness.[14] Abraham and Jacob are literally built up through their trans experiences—both become wealthy patriarchs—but Sarah's actions make her even more miserable. She sees Ishmael as Hagar's son rather than her own,[15] and even though she continues to abuse Hagar, she is forced to watch "the son of that slave woman," as she calls him, grow up as her husband's firstborn heir (Gen. 21:10).[16]

Although Sarah's family situation is unusual, gender failure is a common form of trans experience. Many people, trans or not, know the pain and shame of feeling that we have failed to be the men or women our families, communities, or culture tell us we should be. Often, we experience gender failure as meaning that because we don't fulfill gender expectations, we are not, somehow, "real" men or women. We see such thinking at work in the Babylonian Talmud, where several commentators take Sarah's failure to become a mother as a sign that she was intersex rather than physically female: "Rabbi Nahman stated in the name of Rabbah bar Abbuha: Our mother Sarah was incapable of procreation, for it is said (in Gen. 11:30), 'And Sarai was barren; she had no child.' [That is] she did not even have a place for a fetus, i.e. a womb."[17]

Rabbi Nahman's speculation reflects the way the gender binary fuses, and confuses, gender with biology. Rabbi Nahman recognizes that Sarah does not fulfill the expectation that married women will bear children, but because he doesn't distinguish gender from physical sex, he does not see Sarah's infertility as a form of gender failure, but as a sign that at least in one respect, she was not biologically female.[18]

Sarah ends up blaming Hagar and Abraham for her feelings of gender failure, but when she tells Abraham that God has kept her from bearing, she makes it clear that she sees her condition as imposed on her by God. For Abraham and Jacob, trans experience is a means of securing relationships with God. For Sarah, trans experience is not something she has to go through in order to have a relationship with God, but something God imposes on her. When she tells Abraham that God has made her infertile, she is telling him that she sees her gender failure as a sign—though a painful sign—of God's presence in her life.[19]

That's also the way I see my painful trans experience of growing up with a male body and a female gender identity: as a way God made me. Like many transsexuals, I experienced a double sense of gender failure: I knew I was not a real boy or man, because my gender identity was female, and I knew I could never fit the binary definition of a woman, because I was not born or raised female. I felt, as Sarah felt, that God had given me a body that prevented me from living as the woman I felt I should be. Although my experience of growing up transsexual was different from Sarah's experience of gender failure, I, like Sarah, saw my trans experience as signifying God's presence in my life.

The Torah reports Sarah's belief that God is the cause of her infertility, but it does not confirm that God prevented her from bearing. Like me,

Sarah has nothing but her feelings to support her understanding of her failure to be the woman she is supposed to be. But the Torah leaves no doubt that God is the cause of Sarah's next trans experience, when she conceives and bears a child in old age. God twice announces that Sarah will have a child, and each announcement provokes the same reaction: laughter (Gen. 17:16 and 18:10). When Abraham hears that Sarah will have a child, he literally falls down laughing at the absurdity of elderly people becoming new parents, thinking, "Can a child be born to a man a hundred years old, or can Sarah bear a child at ninety?" (Gen. 17:16). When Sarah hears, she "laugh[s] to herself . . . 'Now that I am withered, am I to have enjoyment—with my husband so old?'" (Gen. 18:12).

Sarah and Abraham laugh when God announces that Sarah will have a child because their understanding of gender—their beliefs about what men and women can do and be—tells them that such a thing is absurd. Abraham laughs at the idea that he and Sarah could have a child at their age; Sarah seems to be laughing at the idea that they will be able to have sex, that she will feel that kind of pleasure (Gen. 18:12). Neither having sex nor having a child is something they expect elderly men and women to do, or be able to do. I know that kind of laughter. The understanding of gender I grew up with made the idea that I could live as a woman after being born and living my whole life as a male seem as absurd to me as the idea that elderly people can become new parents seemed to Abraham and Sarah. When I tried to imagine living as myself, I heard the whole world laughing at me.

The Torah makes it clear that God intends Sarah's pregnancy to provoke this kind of laughter. God could easily have enabled Sarah to have a son when she still was of what we normally think of as childbearing age. If God had done so, Sarah would have been spared decades of gender failure, Hagar would have been spared forced intercourse with Abraham, and the only laughter prompted by Sarah's pregnancy would have been the laughter of pure joy. But such a pregnancy would not have been considered miraculous, a fact the Torah emphasizes by reminding us, the second time Sarah's pregnancy is announced, that "Abraham and Sarah were old, advanced in years; Sarah had stopped having the periods of women" (Gen. 18:11). As God knows, the absurdity of a ninety-year-old woman having a child with a hundred-year-old man is what makes this pregnancy a sign of God's presence. That is presumably why God is not angry when Abraham and Sarah laugh at the news that Sarah will have a child.[20] God means Sarah's pregnancy to provoke that kind of response, which Abraham memorializes by naming their son Isaac, *Yitzhak*, which means "laughter."

Although it is as absurd that Abraham would become a father at a hundred as that Sarah would become a mother at ninety, Abraham's identity was not affected by Sarah's pregnancy. Abraham is already a patriarch and father, and God changes his name and identity before announcing Isaac's birth, in connection with the commandment of circumcision. But as God emphasizes in announcing it to Abraham, Sarah's pregnancy alters who Sarah is: "And God said to Abraham, 'As for your wife Sarai, you shall not call her Sarai, but her name shall be Sarah. I will bless her; indeed, I will give you a son by her. I will bless her so that she shall give rise to nations; rulers of peoples shall issue from her'" (Gen. 17:15–16).

God's focus here is not on the miraculous conception, but on Sarah and God's relationship with her. By changing her name from "Sarai" to "Sarah," God makes it clear that Sarah's identity, no less than Abraham's, is defined by God; by commanding Abraham to call her "Sarah," God shows that who Sarah is to God is more important even than who she is to her husband. By saying, "I will bless her" before and after telling Abraham, "I will give you a son by her," God makes it clear that Sarah's pregnancy is being done not only *to* her but *for* her by God. God is promising Abraham another son, but Sarah's identity—who she is to herself, to her husband, to the world, and to the future forming in her womb—is being utterly transformed.

When Rebekah and Rachel, the other matriarchs who suffer from infertility, finally bear children, they become the kinds of women—mothers— they are expected to be. But instead of helping her fit established gender roles, Sarah's pregnancy makes her a kind of woman who cannot be understood in terms of those roles at all. According to binary definitions, Sarah can either be old woman or a new mother, but not both.[21] By making her a kind of woman who, in terms of gender binary categories, is impossible, Sarah's pregnancy demonstrates God's presence in her life and in the world.

That is also the way I see my transition from living as a man to living as a woman who, according to binary gender, I cannot possibly be: as a miraculous sign of God's presence. Like the elderly, infertile Sarah, before my transition, I had accepted that the life I longed for was a physical and social impossibility, and that I would die without becoming the woman I felt I should be. Like Sarah, I was astonished, doubtful, and afraid when I realized that what I thought was impossible was possible, and that the body that had caused me so much misery could give me the life I had longed for. I, like Sarah, saw God as the source of my gender suffering, and so, like Sarah, I experienced the absurd blossoming of my body—an adolescence in middle age, rather than Sarah's conception in old age—as a divinely given miracle. Every time I look in a mirror and see myself instead of the man I was born to be, I see the power of God.

Traditionally religious people often see transgender people as rebelling not just against gender but against God when we refuse to be the men and women biology and gender tell us we should be. But it is God who makes Sarah a kind of woman who, according to the gender binary, should not exist, and who, as Sarah acknowledges, is not only impossible but absurd: "God has brought me laughter," she says after Isaac is born. "Everyone who hears will laugh [at] me" (Gen. 21:6).[22] Sarah's trans experience of becoming a new mother in old age brings her both *yitzhak*, laughter, the human response to her violation of gender categories, and *Yitzhak*, Isaac, the heir she struggled so long to bear. *Yitzhak*, both the laughter and the boy, attest to the fact that being human in ways that are incomprehensible in terms of binary gender can express God's presence, God's blessing, God's love.

"Take Your Son, Your Favored Son, Whom You Love":
Isaac and the Nightmare of Gender

Isaac's name recalls the laughter provoked by his mother's trans experience of becoming a new mother in old age, but the Torah does not portray Isaac himself as ever being anything other than the boy and man he was born to be. Unlike his parents, Isaac does not need to change or be changed in order to demonstrate God's role in his life: he was born out of a miracle, so his existence attests to God's presence. Circumcision transforms Abraham and Ishmael's identities as males, but Isaac is circumcised when he is eight days old, before he has a male identity to transform. For Abraham, circumcision represents yet another step into the unknown, signifying and sealing his relationship with his invisible, unknowable God. But to Isaac, God is not a mysterious voice from beyond: God is part of the family. And though Isaac, like his son Jacob, is born second, unlike Jacob, Isaac grows up knowing that he will inherit his father's blessing and relationship with God.

From birth to death, Isaac remains the son, heir, husband, father, and patriarch he was born to be. Isaac never leaves his father's house, literally taking his bride, Rebekah (provided for him by his father when he was forty years old), into his mother's tent (Gen. 24:67). The Torah portrays him as an obedient son, a faithful heir who remains within his father's household and inherits his legacy, a monogamous husband, a loving (if foolish) father, and a patriarch who maintains and transmits the relationship with God with which he is entrusted.

But from his conception to his old age, Isaac has his life shaped by his family members' trans experiences. Because God told Abraham to leave his father's house, Isaac grows up without a grandfather. Because God prevented Sarah from conceiving, Hagar, rather than Sarah, bears Abraham's first son, Ishmael; Isaac is not conceived until his mother is elderly; and his position as Abraham's heir is not secure until Sarah, in another fit of God-sanctioned cruelty, demands that Abraham banish Ishmael and Hagar.[23] Unlike his son Jacob, Isaac does nothing to secure the firstborn blessing, but even so, his birthright and blessing, like his son Jacob's, are stolen from his older brother.[24]

The Torah does not describe Isaac's childhood relationship with Ishmael, who is banished after Isaac is weaned.[25] We see Sarah's rage, which flares up after she sees "the son, whom Hagar the Egyptian had born to Abraham, playing," and we hear that Abraham is "distressed . . . greatly" by the idea of banishing Ishmael, "for it concerned a son of his," but the Torah never tells us how Isaac feels about his older brother's disappearance (Gen. 21:9, 11).[26] God assures Abraham that God will protect and "make a nation" of Ishmael, but all the young Isaac knows is that his older brother is gone, demoted from firstborn son to unwanted menace, and driven with his mother into the wilderness (Gen. 21:14).

Even to the young Isaac, it must have been clear that in his family, biology is not destiny. God's presence means that every role and relationship defined by gender is subject to change without notice. Unlike his father, mother, wife, and second-born son, Isaac, in his relationship with God, does not do anything that violates or transforms the gender roles he was born to. But as Sarah's gender failure shows, devotion to being the women or men we are supposed to be can also lead to trans experience. In one of the most horrifying stories in the Torah, traditionally called the Akedah, or "binding of Isaac," God turns Isaac's firstborn role upside down, so that his position as beloved son and heir makes him the target of his father's divinely ordered violence:

> Some time afterward, God put Abraham to the test. [God] said to him, "Abraham," and he answered, "Here I am." And [God] said, "Take your son, your favored one, Isaac, whom you love, and go to the land of Moriah, and offer him there as a burnt offering." . . . So early next morning, Abraham saddled his ass and took with him two of his servants and his son Isaac. He split the wood for the burnt offering, and he set out for the place of which God had told him. On the third day Abraham looked up and saw the place from afar. Then Abraham said to his servants, "You stay here with the ass. The boy and I will go up there: we will worship and we will return to you." Abraham took the wood for the burnt offering and put it on his son Isaac. He himself took the firestone and the knife; the two walked off together. Then Isaac said to his father Abraham, "Father!" And he answered, "Yes, my son." And he said, "Here are the firestone and the wood; but where is the sheep for the burnt offering?" And Abraham said, "God will see to the sheep for [the] burnt offering, my son." And the two of them walked on together. They arrived at the place of which God had told him. Abraham built an altar there; he laid out the wood; he bound his son Isaac; he laid him on the altar, on top of the wood. And Abraham picked up the knife to slay his son. (Gen. 22:1–10)

The Akedah begins the way Isaac's life story begins, with Abraham hearing the voice of God. But this time, instead of foretelling Isaac's birth, God commands his death. By identifying Isaac as "your son, your favored one, . . . whom you love," God makes it clear that this test requires Abraham to put obedience to God ahead of his fatherly love for Isaac and his patriarchal devotion to preserving the life of his heir. In fact, God's command turns those values upside down: Abraham is supposed to kill Isaac *because* Isaac is his beloved son and heir.

But throughout this ordeal, Isaac remains the obedient, faithful son. He follows his father into the wilderness without asking where or why they are going or when they will arrive or return. He makes no objection when Abraham leaves their donkey and the servants who have accompanied them and forces Isaac to carry the wood for the sacrificial fire (Gen. 22:5–6). When, after several days of walking, Isaac breaks his silence to ask "where is the sheep for the burnt offering?," he accepts his father's mysterious assurance that "God will see . . . to the burnt offering" without further question (Gen. 22:7–8). When his father prepares him to be sacrificed, Isaac allows himself to be bound to the altar without a word of protest (Gen. 22:9). Other than his single question, Isaac does nothing but what his father tells him to do. He goes where his father goes, carries what his father gives him to carry, lies down on the altar his father builds, lies still in the bonds with which his father binds him.

As faithful as Abraham is to God, Isaac is faithful to gender. Isaac probably isn't thinking about gender as he lies there on the altar, but the Torah makes sure we remember that gender is what brought him there, repeating the words "son" and "boy" twelve times in nineteen verses. Like me before my transition, Isaac is determined to live as the male he is supposed to be even if it kills him; during the Akedah, for Isaac, as for me, life as a male becomes a form of self-destruction.

But the Akedah is not presented as a story about Isaac; it is a story about Abraham and whether he will put his devotion to God ahead of his devotion to his son and the future his son represents. Abraham passes this terrible test. His binding of Isaac leads to what must have seemed to him a happy ending: as he lifts the knife, he secures God's blessings without having to kill his son:

> An angel of the LORD called to him from heaven: "Abraham! Abraham!" And he answered, "Here I am." And [the angel] said, "Do not raise your hand against the boy, or do anything to him. For

now I know that you fear God, since you have not withheld your son, your favored one, from Me." When Abraham looked up, his eye fell upon a ram, caught in the thicket by its horns. So Abraham went and took the ram and offered it up as a burnt offering in place of his son. . . . The angel of the LORD called to Abraham a second time from heaven, and said, "By Myself I swear, the LORD declares: because you have done this and have not withheld your son, your favored one, I will bestow My blessing upon you and make your descendants as numerous as the stars of heaven and the sands on the seashore; and your descendants shall seize the gates of their foes. All the nations of the earth shall bless themselves by your descendants, because you have obeyed My command." (Gen. 22:11–18)

God rewards Abraham by protecting the son and posterity that Abraham was about to sacrifice, and promising a torrent of future blessings. These blessings, like the blessings God promises when first commanding Abraham to leave his father's house, make it clear that God's covenant with Abraham is founded on Abraham's willingness to violate his assigned gender roles.[27] Religious traditionalists often claim that the Torah shows that God requires us to do what gender says men and women should do, but Jewish and other Abrahamic religions wouldn't exist if Abraham had refused God's commands and insisted on acting as the devoted son and loving father he was supposed to be.

The end of the Akedah is so focused on Abraham and God that it completely ignores Isaac. In the ten verses leading up to this scene, Isaac is named five times; in these verses, he is referred to as "the boy," "your son," and "your favored one," but his name is not mentioned once. After the angel interrupts the sacrifice, we are told that Abraham notices and sacrifices a ram, but the Torah does not say when, or whether, Isaac is unbound from the altar, what he does after he is released, or how he feels about what his father and God have done, and almost done, to him (Gen. 22:13).

I don't need a description of Isaac's feelings to know that when Abraham attempts to sacrifice him, Isaac endures a traumatic form of trans experience. During the Akedah, Isaac learns what his older brother Ishmael and countless LGBTQ people have learned: that gender itself can become a nightmare, turning family members into mortal enemies who see us not as cherished children, siblings, parents, or spouses but as creatures that must be sacrificed, a nightmare in which we cannot even cry out to God, because it is God, we are told, who demands that we be targeted.

As Isaac's experience shows, it is not only those who do not fit our assigned gender roles who find ourselves bound on gender's altar. Wives who are taught to "stand by" the men who abuse them, young men who submit to violence in order to "prove their manhood," women who starve themselves or vomit to achieve ideals of female beauty, men who believe that they, like Abraham, must repress or betray their deepest feelings— many people, in one way or another, experience gender as a nightmare in which the pressure to be the men or women we are supposed to be leads us to destruction.[28]

Even when we survive it, the nightmare of gender can wound us for the rest of our lives. After the Akedah, Isaac seems unchanged. He continues to fulfill his role as Abraham's favored son and heir, remaining in his father's household, marrying the woman his father finds for him, and, after his father's death, inheriting his father's possessions and relationship with God. But the intimacy we glimpse when Isaac, with absolute trust, says to his father, "Here are the fire and the wood; but where is the sheep for the burnt offering?," seems to have been sacrificed, along with the ram caught in the thicket, on Mount Moriah. Isaac lives with his father until Abraham's death at age 175, but after Isaac asks that question, the Torah does not record a single instance in which father and son speak to one another. After Abraham's death, the Torah tells us, "God blessed his son Isaac" (Gen. 25:11), but there is no scene in which Abraham gives his son his innermost blessing, as Isaac does when he feels that the end of his life is near.[29] And though Isaac and Ishmael faithfully bury the father who betrayed them, the Torah does not report that either mourned him.

Isaac's relationship with God also seems damaged by the Akedah. Isaac does what God tells him to do, but as with his father, Isaac obeys in silence. Three times, God blesses Isaac; three times, Isaac says nothing in response (Gen. 25:11, 26:3–4, 26:23). When God tells Isaac not to go to Egypt during a famine, Isaac obeys without question or comment (Gen.

26:1–6). When God appears to Isaac in Beersheba and tells him not to be afraid, Isaac builds "an altar there and invoke[s] the LORD by name," but though he "invokes" God, the Torah does not record Isaac as speaking *to* God (Gen. 26:23–25).[30]

Whatever wounds are expressed by Isaac's silence, he remains faithful to the patriarchal system that nearly cost him his life, fulfilling his roles as son, husband, and father no matter what befalls him. Isaac's faithfulness to gender sets him apart from both his family and the God who, in one way or another, leads Isaac's father, mother, brother, wife, and second-born son beyond the gender roles they were born to.[31]

God's disruptions of gender in these stories make it clear that even the gender roles that matter most to human beings are not sacred to God. Indeed, God not only blesses Abraham for violating his roles as son and father, but blesses all his descendants. Yet however God warps and wrenches gender roles, the blessings given at the end of the Akedah make it clear that God does not do so in order to undermine gender. To make good on the promise to multiply Abraham's descendants, God needs Abraham and his descendants to maintain patriarchal gender roles and values. If fathers don't pass God's blessing and covenant onto their sons, if later generations do not identify themselves as children of Abraham, then the nations of the earth won't be able to bless themselves by Abraham's descendants, because no one will know who Abraham's descendants are.

In other words, God in the Torah uses gender, but is not bound by it. On the one hand, God depends on gender to transmit the covenant across time and space, so that even after hundreds of generations, Jews will still see themselves as children of Abraham. On the other hand, God disrupts gender as a way of making God's power and presence known, requiring Abraham and Jacob to violate their assigned gender roles in order to secure relationships with God, preventing Sarah from bearing children until she is elderly, and decreeing that God's blessing be passed on to second-born sons (Isaac and Jacob) rather than firstborn sons (Ishmael and Esau).

The Torah presents gender as a means to God's ends, to be reinforced or disrupted as God pleases. God could easily have commanded Abraham to take his elderly father with him in his wanderings, allowed Sarah to have children when she was of childbearing age, and ensured that Jacob rather than Esau emerged first from Rebekah's womb. But in these stories, faithfulness to gender has little to do with faithfulness to God. In fact, God counts on the fact that people are not bound by gender roles. The covenant with Abraham is founded on Abraham, Sarah, and Jacob's embrace of trans experience: their willingness to live outside the gender roles they were born to and become the kinds of people that they are not supposed to be. By portraying trans experience as the foundation for the covenant with Abraham, the Torah plants God's recognition that people do not have to be what binary gender says we are at the heart of Abrahamic religious traditions.

From the time I started reading the Torah, I have found it comforting that God, like me, does not make sense in terms of binary gender. That made me feel less lonely when I was a child; later, when I lost my marriage, my home, my job, and many of my friendships, it reassured me to know that my relationship with God would not be disrupted or threatened by my gender transition. To many of the people who knew me as a man, my transition meant that I was betraying my roles as husband, father, and son, wearing strange clothes and talking in a strange voice, becoming someone who did not make sense in terms of gender. But to God, I knew, I was becoming what I had always been, growing into the person God, for reasons I will never understand, created me to be. Although my human relationships ended or changed when I stopped living as a man, my relationship with God was undisturbed: we knew and loved one another as we always had, whispering in the wilderness beyond gender.

But even if gender doesn't matter much to God, as we see in the Akedah, gender does matter to human beings. Family gender roles define the ways we should and shouldn't treat one another, the responsibilities we are expected to shoulder and the responsibilities we can count on others to shoulder for us, our duties to care for one another and our expectations that we will be cared for in return. When Abraham follows God's command to murder his son, he enters a moral wilderness, where God, as invisibly, inhumanly present as magnetic north, is the only point on the compass.[32] But however God might judge Abraham's actions, to Isaac, Abraham is his father, a man Isaac trusts and obeys without question because, according to gender, he can count on his father to protect and care for him. For Isaac, Abraham's willingness to step outside the role of father does not make him a liberating example of the ways God can lead us beyond gender; it makes him a monster.

My transition from living as a man to living as myself didn't lead me to abandon or assault my children, but like Isaac, my children were also hurt when I stopped acting like the father they loved and trusted. Transition, to me, meant becoming the person God created me to be; to my children, it meant that I, like Abraham, was betraying my responsibilities as father for reasons they could not understand. Unlike Isaac, my children continued to speak with their father who did not act like a father, but like Isaac's relationship with Abraham, their relationships with me have been wounded ever after.

Don't get me wrong: gender transition is not child abuse. Unlike Abraham, I did not set out to hurt my children, and unlike Abraham, I have never stopped caring for and protecting them. But because my children's relationships with me were so bound up in gender, it was impossible for me to become myself without disrupting their lives, or to keep them from feeling hurt and betrayed by the father they expected not only to love them but to always be a man.

Modern commentators often read the Akedah as a story not of Abraham's triumph but of his failure. Pointing to a rabbinic commentary that portrays Abraham as misunderstanding God's command—according to Rabbi Abba, God told Abraham not to kill Isaac but only to lift him up, the literal meaning of *olah*, "sacrifice"—many argue that Abraham actually fails God's test because in being willing to sacrifice Isaac, he sacrifices, and believes God wants him to sacrifice, human standards of morality.[33] According to this view, God hoped that Abraham would reject God's command, and reject any relationship with God that would require him to kill his son.[34]

But whether or not we believe that God's command was misunderstood by Abraham, God lets the sacrifice continue until Abraham has bound Isaac on the altar and is about to cut his throat. Abraham may or may not fail God, but God certainly fails Abraham and Isaac by commanding or allowing Abraham to violate the moral bonds that are supposed to bind fathers to sons.

Before my gender transition, I tried to be a good father, a good husband, a good man. Binary gender told me what being a good man meant, what roles and responsibilities I had to fulfill, what I should and shouldn't do. When I stopped living as a man, it was clear that no matter what new life I made, by binary standards, I was a bad father, a bad husband, a bad man. But binary gender couldn't tell me what it meant to be a good transgender person. It offered no roles for me to play, no responsibilities to shoulder, no guide to what I must or must not do.

As far as gender was concerned, once I stopped living as a man, I had entered a moral wilderness. I had to decide for myself what it meant to be a good transgender person, parent, partner, and ex-partner, and I had to hold myself to those values, because no one in my family or community knew what they were. Slowly, I learned to find my way through that wilderness: to be guided by love rather than duty, to be true to my own sense of goodness rather than looking to binary ideas of what good men or good women should be.

Throughout this journey, I have been encouraged by the ways in which the Torah links trans experience to relationship with God. When I read the stories of Abraham, Sarah, Isaac, and Jacob, the Torah reassures me that trans experiences can grow out of, bear witness to, and strengthen our relationship with God; every time the Torah refers to God as the God of Abraham, Isaac, and Jacob, it helps me remember that even trans experiences that cut us off from other people can connect us to God.

But the horror of the Akedah reminds us that relationship with God is not enough. When we enter the wilderness of possibility beyond the gender roles we have been born to, it is up to us to maintain the moral values that are normally bound up with those roles: to be faithful even when we are seen by others as betrayers; to take care of those who depend on us even when they feel we have abandoned them; to be good even when we are seen as evil; to be loving even when we are objects of hatred; to hold ourselves to the highest standards even when others don't value us at all. God made me transgender, but as Abraham's example shows, even when it is God who leads us into the wilderness, it is up to us to decide what it means to be human.

THREE

CLOSE ENCOUNTERS WITH AN INCOMPREHENSIBLE GOD

Wendy, Maimonides, and Me

When I was in fourth grade, I walked home from school almost every day with a girl named Wendy.[1] Wendy was smart, bookish, and not afraid to speak her mind. I felt closer to Wendy than I had ever felt to another human being. We didn't play together, we talked, and as we swung our empty lunch boxes under the flaming maples, I could almost believe that I was just a girl with another girl, that I was seen and known, and had somehow magically become who I really was.

But I knew I was pretending. Wendy couldn't see me as a girl. She could only see me in the terms the little sliver of world we were walking through had taught us to use to make sense of human beings. In many ways, those terms brought us together, helping us recognize how alike we were: pale, freckled, curly-haired kids in the same grade, bookworms who preferred reading and talking to almost every other activity, members of families who lived in houses, and, though I never thought about it, people who were white.

Wendy and I seemed so much alike that grown-ups sometimes mistook us for siblings. But I felt closer to Wendy than to anyone in my family—and closer to being myself when I was with her than with any other human being.

But no matter how similar we seemed, in terms of binary gender, we were absolutely different. There was only one girl walking home under the maples. The other child, to Wendy and to everyone else, was a boy named Jay.

As the leaves fell and disappeared beneath upstate New York snow, I imagined telling Wendy who I really was. The snowbanks melted; the trees budded. Night after night, I fantasized that tomorrow would be the day when some miracle would enable Wendy to see the invisible girl haunting my boy-body. Our lunch boxes swung; the grass turned green; our shadows, almost identical in the warming sun, tangled and fused and disappeared in the deepening maple shade. When the school year ended, Wendy moved away to another state.

Why didn't I come out to Wendy? She was not only smart and thoughtful, she was also the daughter of anthropologists (though I'm not sure I knew what that meant). But even if I said to her, "Wendy, I'm really a girl," I knew that in our world that couldn't be true. Being a girl meant having a female body; no one with a male body could "really" be a girl. I could have told her I was "transsexual"—I had learned that word—but I couldn't have explained what transsexual meant. The idea of gender as something distinct from sex was just beginning to be developed in the faraway grown-up world of feminists and psychological researchers, and if I had heard of sex, it was as something dirty, something my parents didn't want me to know about.

But even if I could have explained the difference between gender and gender identity and physical sex, telling Wendy that I was a transsexual wouldn't have been the same as showing her that I was a girl like her. In fact, I would have been revealing that not only wasn't I like her, but I wasn't like anyone either of us knew: I was different in ways that made me other than male or female, boy or girl, something that didn't make sense in the terms that defined her and everyone else we knew. If I let her keep seeing me as a boy, I could continue being her best friend, but if I didn't, I was sure our friendship would be over. If Wendy realized how strange I was, she would see me as a stranger. To come out to Wendy would be to come out not as someone even more like her than she thought, but as someone who didn't fit the terms of humanity, as someone who, though I didn't know the word then, was what I would now call *queer*.

I knew only one other person who was queer, and that person—God—was much, much queerer than I was.

Unlike Wendy, God saw through my body, and understood what and who I was even though I couldn't explain it. God loved all of me, not just the male persona Wendy called her friend. But though in many ways I felt closer to God than to Wendy, God and I didn't have much in common. I had a body that concealed who I was; God had no body at all. Even though my body hid my female gender identity from Wendy, having human bodies meant we were alike in many ways. Unlike God, Wendy and I were both born, grew, breathed, ate, laughed, slept, and moved from one place and moment to another. Our hearts beat, our stomachs growled, we felt lonely and happy and angry and afraid, we remembered pasts and imagined futures and dwelt in the bubble of now that shimmered between them. God didn't play, eat, watch TV, sleep, get bored, or ride a bike, and even though God was always there, God wasn't there the way Wendy and I were. When I was lying in bed talking with God, I wasn't anywhere else, but God wasn't just there with me, God was . . . I didn't know where. God didn't seem to have a where. God was inside me and all around me and also, though this was very hard to imagine, completely beyond me, existing in places and times and ways that had nothing to do with me.

God never talked to me the way God talks with people in the Torah, didn't split seas for me or work other nature-disrupting miracles for my benefit, but otherwise, the God I saw in the Torah seemed basically the same as the God I knew in my life: invisible, bodiless, everywhere and nowhere, alive and present but not in ways that made sense in human terms. One minute, God is creating the world, the next, God is destroying it with a flood. On this page, God promises Sarah and Abraham a son; a few pages later, God tells Abraham to kill that son. That was the God I knew—a loving, dangerous, incomprehensible God who kept me from killing myself one night and woke me the next morning to a life I couldn't bear to live. I made no sense in terms of binary gender; God made no sense in human terms at all.

When I was growing up, I generally assumed that God, like my gender, was something I couldn't talk about with other people, but I did have one conversation about God. My family was camping, as we called it—staying in a fold-out tent hauled by our powder-blue Ford to a campground filled with mosquitoes, families, trailers, and fire pits. My father loved to sit by the campfire at night, strumming the guitar he never played at home and singing folk songs he had learned—my mother recently revealed—so that he could attract girls. ("It worked with me," she said.)

On this camping trip—I must have been eleven or twelve—the people singing around the fire included a man who had some kind of professional involvement with Judaism. My parents, who, apart from my father's occasional insistence that God was nothing more than wishful thinking, rarely talked about religion, encouraged me to talk with him.

As though he had been waiting to do so, the man rose from the campfire. We picked our way between legs and marshmallow-laden sticks and headed into the darkness. Soon we had left trailers, campfires, and electric lights behind, and were following his bobbing flashlight beam along a dirt path overhung by trees that led around a lake. The dark, thick with branches and insects, was barely diluted by the moonlight splashing off the thicker darkness of the lake.

I don't remember how our conversation started, but it wasn't long before we were talking about God. How, I asked him, over and over, posing the question in every way I could think of, could God be all-powerful, all-knowing, all-good, and so on, and still allow the Holocaust, not to mention all the other suffering in the world?

It was thrilling to be able to talk about God and I was flattered by his attention, but I was also very bored. I didn't care about the questions I was asking. I knew that God was God, no matter what human beings suffered or did to one another. The terms I was using—words like "omnipresent," "infinite," and "eternal"—made God seem like an idea that could be logically worked out instead of a living presence. That wasn't the way I experienced God. God wasn't all-good, all-this, or all-that; God just was.

Although the man's smooth, deep voice was unfailingly patient, I could tell that he too was bored. I wonder now if I sold him short. Maybe he would have been interested if had I come clean about my relationship with God; maybe he would have understood. But I never considered doing that. God and I met in a wilderness that I was sure he and all the other men and women who identified with their bodies and lives that went with them couldn't imagine, a wilderness where God and I could recognize one another without forms, hold one another without arms, be present to one another without needing to be visible to anyone else. Because my relationship with God seemed as incomprehensible as my relationship with gender, I betrayed God the way I constantly betrayed my female gender identity: I pretended to be someone I wasn't, presenting myself as a kind of Jew, one searching for faith and struggling with belief, I was sure the man would recognize and understand.

I can't remember his name, but I can still see him when I close my eyes: tall, broad-shouldered, clean-shaven, with short hair and a square jaw. He didn't, as we say, "look Jewish," but he definitely looked male, at ease in his body, his clothes, his heterosexuality, his place in the mid-1960s American version of the gender binary. To be human, I thought, was to fit that binary. He was clearly human. God and I were not.

Now that I know I *am* human, I know that despite his comfort with being a man, he must not have completely fit the terms of binary gender either, because he, like me, was made in the image of God, and so he, like me, was more than human terms can comprehend.

When I was growing up, my father liked to tell me that human beings create God in our own image. I didn't think much about it then, because to my father, I knew, God was just an idea, and not a very good one. But now I realize that my father was right. Although I experience God as a living presence, because I think and talk about God in human terms, my conception of God reflects my conception of humanity—so when I thought that humanity did not include me, my conception of God was based on the ways in which God, like me, was inhuman.

My father would probably have seen my acknowledgment that my conception of God reflected my conception of humanity as yet another sign (for him there were many) that there is no God, only words that we mistake for God. Like other people, I am imagining God in my own image, and then telling myself God *is* the things I say to myself about God. Judith Plaskow has a more optimistic interpretation. Although she would agree with my father that our conceptions of God are always rooted in and limited by our conceptions of humanity, for her, that means that when we expand our definition of humanity, we have the chance—Plaskow would say the obligation—to expand our conceptions of God, to understand God in terms of the perspectives and experiences of people we previously ignored or excluded from our idea of what it means to be human.[2]

But even though I have expanded my definition of humanity to include people who, like me, do not fit the terms of binary gender, God seems as queer to me as ever—inhuman, incomprehensible, unlike anything I can say or know. Although it is only recently that people have begun to refer to God as queer, there is a long theological tradition, often called "negative theology," devoted to the idea that God cannot be described or understood in human terms. For example, the great medieval rabbi, philosopher, and physician Moses Maimonides spends many pages of his *Guide for the Perplexed* teaching his readers to recognize what I would call God's absolute queerness—God's absolute difference from human beings.

Although Maimonides, unlike my father, believes that there is a God who has nothing to do with what we say or think about God, like my father, Maimonides is dismayed by the tendency of religious texts and people to describe God in human terms; like my father, he is skeptical and scornful of the conceptions of God implied by those descriptions; and like my father, Maimonides sees conceptions of God in human terms as both empty and deceptive, reflections not of God but of human limitations and self-centeredness. But unlike my father, Maimonides believes we can and must free ourselves from these conceptions, by reminding ourselves that the only thing we know about God is that God is not like anything we know: "There is absolutely no likeness in any respect whatever between [God] and the things created by [God]; [God's] existence has no likeness to theirs; nor [God's] life to the life of those among them who are alive."[3]

Had Maimonides been able to intervene in my childhood relationship with God, he would no doubt have told me that I was wrong to identify with God as a fellow outsider to human roles and categories, because, as he says here, there is no similarity between God and God's creatures. Unlike God's, my difference from others, Maimonides would have told me, was not absolute; despite my queerness in terms of gender, I was basically similar to other human beings.[4] My body was a human body; my life was a human life; even my feelings of difference and isolation were common human feelings. My sense that God and I were similar in our invisibility and incomprehensibility reflected my naiveté and lack of philosophical sophistication. Like those who imagine God as a man with a long white beard, I was imagining God in humanizing terms that made God seem closer, more comprehensible. "You are God's creature," my imaginary Maimonides would say, "and as God's creature, you have nothing in common with your Creator."

Maimonides was as great a doctor as he was a thinker; I hope he would not have prescribed a rigorous diet of negative theology to a suicidal child who felt close to no one but God, because I am not sure that I or my relationship with God could have survived his instruction.[5] Would I still have felt God's presence if I had constantly reminded myself that everything I thought about God was wrong? Would I still have poured out my heart to God if I knew, really knew, that God and I had nothing in common?

But whether or not Maimonides's critique of the way I thought about God would have been good for me at the time, Maimonides would have been right. Other people couldn't recognize or understand my female gender identity, but, compared with our absolute difference from God, we were all basically similar creatures. No matter how different I felt, the gulf that separated me from Wendy and other humans was nothing compared to the gulf between me and God.

Had Maimonides taught me the principles of his negative theology, he would have made sure I knew not only that God was nothing like me, but also that every word I used for God was wrong. God, Maimonides insists, cannot be described in language, even the language of the Torah. Language works by implying similarity, but God is One, unique, unlike anything else in any way.[6] According to Maimonides, the terms in which I thought of God when I was a child were not only inaccurate, they also betrayed the very queerness that made me feel so close to God, by implying that God is queer the way I am queer, instead of acknowledging that God is absolutely queer, utterly different from me and everything I knew.[7]

Although I wouldn't have understood the intricacies of Maimonides's theology when I was a child, I think I would have realized he was right that my words misrepresented God. I told myself that God was there, but I knew God wasn't there the way I was, present in one place and time and not in any other. I told myself God understood me, but I knew that God understood me in a way that was unimaginably different from the way I knew myself. I couldn't have explained it the way Maimonides does, but I understood that the words I used for God didn't describe God: they were only gestures, waving from the patch of life I knew toward a vastness I could never understand.

But even though I knew my words for God completely misrepresented God, I went on using that language, for the same reason that I never stopped Wendy from talking to me as though I were a boy: no matter how badly human terms misrepresented us, Wendy needed them to relate to me, and I needed them to relate to God.

Maimonides would disagree. He sees the refusal to use words for God as a sign of the highest degree of spiritual and philosophical development. To Maimonides, as to many philosophers and theologians, the closer we come to God, the more overpowered we are by awareness that God is beyond our capacity for knowledge or understanding. The closest we can come to expressing that truth is silence.[8]

While I agree with Maimonides that words cannot help but misrepresent God, I have never reached this exalted level. As a child, I needed words for God, and I need them now. I need to say, "God is here, God sees me, God understands me, God loves me, God hears my cry, and God answers." Even if I swore off using any other human terms for God, I, like Maimonides, would still need to say, "God is." I don't say these things as meaningless pointers toward a truth I cannot understand. I say them because I mean them, because even though they are not and cannot be true of God, they are true to my experience of God, and I can't relate to God without them.

Footsteps in the Garden: God in Human Terms

Even though I, like other people, used language to relate to God when I was a child, I told myself that because I met God in the wilderness outside gender categories, I understood God in ways that other people, even the people who interact with God in the Torah, do not. From the moment Adam is created, the Torah shows human beings speaking intimately with God. But to me it seemed that just as Wendy could only relate to me by thinking of me as someone who, like her, fit binary gender categories, the people in the Torah could only relate to God by thinking of God as someone who, like them, has a body that locates and limits God in space and time. That is certainly the way Adam and Eve relate to God after they eat the fruit of the Tree of the Knowledge of Good and Evil:

> Then the eyes of both of them were opened and they perceived that they were naked; and they sewed together fig leaves and made themselves loincloths.

They heard the sound of the LORD God moving about in the garden at the breezy time of day; and the man and his wife hid from the LORD God among the trees of the garden. The LORD God called out to the man and said to him, "Where are you?" He replied, "I heard the sound of You in the garden, and I was afraid because I was naked, so I hid." (Gen. 3:7–9)

The commentaries in the copy of the Torah I read as a child noted that this passage portrays God anthropomorphically, not only in human terms but also, like a human being, as noisily moving through a specific part of the Garden at a specific time. (Those commentaries probably taught me the word "anthropomorphism.") If we take this portrayal of God literally, it raises significant theological problems. How could the God who two chapters before created the universe be noisily and blindly wandering through a tiny part of that creation?

If we read this passage the way Maimonides reads the Torah's anthropomorphic descriptions of God, we see it as a reflection of human nature rather than divine nature: the Torah, Maimonides says, deliberately presents God in humanizing terms that make God accessible to everyone, even the most unsophisticated. I also saw the physical descriptions of God in this story as reflections of human beings' inability to imagine a God who didn't have a body, but I didn't see the Torah as trying to make God seem human. The Torah doesn't describe God as moving noisily in the Garden; it tells us that that is how Eve and Adam perceived God. As Genesis 3:7 makes clear, after eating the forbidden fruit, Adam and Eve identify themselves with their bodies in a new way: their nakedness suddenly makes them feel exposed and ashamed, leading them to cover their genitals and to believe that hiding their bodies among the trees will hide them from God. They not only identify themselves with their bodies; as I noticed when I read this passage as a child, they think the same way about God, perceiving God as moving like a person with a body from one place to another, and being unable to find them through the trees.

Just as I let Wendy see me as a boy because she couldn't see me any other way, I saw God as playing along with Eve and Adam in this scene, asking "Where are you?" as though God, like them, could only be in one place at a time, and couldn't know where they were until they showed themselves. God, I thought, was doing what I did every day: pretending to have a body to be close to people who needed to imagine God as being like them in order to realize that God was there, in the little patch of space and time to which human beings defined by human bodies are limited.

But even as I condescended to Eve and Adam's need to think of God as being like them, as Maimonides and my father no doubt would have told me, I was doing the same thing, reading God's acceptance of their need to perceive God in physical terms as a sign that God and I felt the same combination of love, loneliness, and despair. Both God and I, I thought, could only be close to human beings by pretending to be what we weren't, masking ourselves in human terms that made us visible to others by hiding who we really were.

It was depressing to think that God, like me, had to sacrifice honesty for intimacy with human beings. But for me, as for Adam and Eve, thinking of God as sharing my limitations made God seem closer, more present, like someone I could count on to find me no matter how completely I was hidden. Adam and Eve, acutely aware of their bodies after eating the fruit, perceive God in ways that reflect their feelings about themselves. I, acutely aware of my inability to form relationships in which I was known and loved for who I was, perceived in God as someone who, like me, could not create relationships with human beings in which God was recognized as God, as though God were as lonely as I was, stranded outside the human world, longing to get in.

Imagining God in terms of my isolation as a trans child helped me feel close to God, but, like other forms of anthropomorphism, it also made it harder to recognize my actual relationship with God. God and I could meet in the wilderness not because I, as a trans child, was special, but because I, like other human beings, was created in God's image, and so I, like other human beings, could never completely fit human categories.

I found it hard to recognize that as a child. I felt so different from other people that I didn't think about what we had in common. And though I didn't want to be different (I wanted to be a normal girl), because I *was* different, I wanted to believe that my difference made me closer to God.

If I hadn't been so invested in that belief—if I had realized that, as

Maimonides would have told me, my difference from other people was not, like God's, absolute—I might have noticed that, as we saw in chapter 2, the Torah offers a number of examples of non-transgender people who stop acting like the men and women they are supposed to be and follow God into the wilderness beyond their assigned gender roles. But because I was reading the Torah through the lens of the despair I felt as a closeted trans child, I only noticed—only wanted to notice—the moments in the Torah when relationships with God fail to overcome human beings' need to imagine God as having a body.

And so, I paid much more attention to Adam and Eve's misperception of God in the Garden than to the intimacy we see a few verses later, when God, understanding the sense of nakedness and vulnerability that comes from identifying with their bodies, clothes Eve and Adam in garments of skin that God has made for them (Gen. 3:21). I gave a cynical, self-satisfied sigh when I read about the Israelites making and worshipping the Golden Calf at Mount Sinai a few weeks after hearing God give the Ten Commandments, but glossed over the make-up scene in which God responds to Moses's longing to know God better by promising, with self-anthropomorphizing tenderness, "I will put you in a cleft of the rock and shield you with My hand until I have passed by. Then I will take My hand away and you will see my back" (Exod. 33:22–23). In both of those scenes, God not only accepts the human need to relate to God in physical terms, but also embraces physicality—clothing Eve and Adam's nakedness, shielding Moses with a hand and letting Moses see something he can take for the body of God—as a way to express God's presence, God's closeness, God's intimate involvement with human lives, and God's commitment to being known by human beings even in terms that misrepresent the God they enable us to glimpse.

God in Human Terms

As long as I lived as a male, the way I read the Torah was shaped by my insistence on seeing God as someone who, like me, couldn't be known by the people we loved. When I began living my transgender identity and forming relationships in which I was seen as who I was, the way I read the Torah slowly began to change. But when I returned to teaching at my Orthodox Jewish university as myself after receiving tenure as a man and one of my students asked, "How has gender transition affected the way you read the Torah?," I didn't yet have an answer.

At that time, I had only been living as a woman for a year. My body was just beginning to feel like mine, like me. I finally identified with the face I saw in the mirror, but I still froze before I looked, afraid that somehow, between trips to the bathroom, I might once again have vanished. Day by day, interaction by interaction, I began to trust that I wasn't disembodied or invisible anymore, that I, like other people, was really there, that when someone looked in my direction, they were seeing me, the real me, the me I had always hidden. Others might not understand what it meant for me to identify myself as female after living for decades as a man, but they could see that I—me as I knew myself to be—was there. Even though my lifelong fears of rejection were realized in some relationships, in others I was accepted, even by people who, like most of my students, didn't know what to make of me in terms of gender.

In other words, gender transition changed the aspects of my life that had made me feel so distant from humanity and so close to God. I still felt close to God, but that feeling was no longer based on imagining that God shared my closeted isolation. Now I saw God as the one who brought me out of the depths of despair, who split the binary sea of gender and led me across on dry land, who made the impossible—me—a reality.

By changing the way I related to God and to the people around me, gender transition was, as my student assumed, changing the way I read the Torah. Instead of focusing on moments when God was misunderstood by human beings, I paid more attention to the stories in which, as I discussed in chapter 2, relationships with God led people to live in ways that are very different from the gender roles they were born to. When I read these stories in the midst of my own life-changing gender disruption, for the first time in my Torah-reading life, I found myself identifying less with God and more with the human characters, particularly Abraham.[9] As I noted in chapter 2, I suddenly saw Abraham as a kindred spirit, a father who, like me, overturns his life and family to become the person he needs to become.

Although my identification with Abraham was based on the ways we had both abandoned our assigned gender roles, once I started paying attention to him, I couldn't help but notice his intimacy with God—an intimacy that defies my childhood assumption that human beings can't relate to anyone who doesn't make sense in human terms. From the moment God—invisible, bodiless, and nameless—tells Abraham to leave his father's house, Abraham recognizes and responds to God without trying to understand or identify God in human terms. He doesn't ask God for a name or proof of God's power or authority, nor, as Adam and Eve do in the Garden, does he try to locate God in time and space or imagine God's voice as coming from a body. He listens to and obeys a God he cannot see or comprehend, a God who has no religion, no presence in myth or history, no previous connection with his family, a God who tells him to do things that make no sense—abandon his father, uproot his wife, trade the man he has been for whatever it is the God he follows into the wilderness is summoning him to become—in return for a reward that makes no sense: blessings that will be showered on the distant descendants of children that Abraham, in his seventies, has not yet fathered. But Abraham, like Maimonides's ideal philosopher, does not try to make sense of God: he silently accepts whatever God is and does whatever God says.

Abraham's willingness to accept a God who makes no sense in human terms is the basis for his relationship with God.[10] He doesn't know why God chose him, or why God tells him to leave his father and sacrifice his son, and he doesn't ask. To Abraham, God is whatever God is and will be whatever God will be. Maybe that's why, though the Torah tells us that Abraham "invokes the LORD by name" (Gen. 12:8), it doesn't portray him as ever talking about God, even to Sarah, Ishmael, and Isaac, whose lives are repeatedly upended by God's commands. Abraham keeps as silent about God as Maimonides recommends, as though his encounters with God have taught him that he cannot know anything about what God is or what God may do next.[11]

Maimonides makes it sound as though God can either be misrepresented and misunderstood in human terms, or not be represented, written, or talked about at all. That's the way I used to think of binary gender: I could present myself in gendered terms that hid who I really was, or I couldn't present myself at all. But once I began living as myself, I found that my relation to binary gender was more complicated than that. Even though I don't fit binary definitions of female, I present myself as a woman. Presenting myself as a woman fosters my relationships with others by making my female gender identification visible, offering others familiar ways to understand and relate to me, ways that make sense to them even if they don't understand or accept the idea that someone born and raised male can "be" a woman.

The Torah portrays God as having a similarly complicated relation to human terms. Sometimes, as in God's first call to Abraham, God, invisible and incomprehensible, presents simply as God, but sometimes, as when God asks "Where are you?" in the Garden, God chooses to present in human terms, embracing misrepresentation for the sake of relationship, just as I do when I present in binary gender terms. In fact, at the beginning of Genesis 18, God embraces human terms so completely that even Abraham mistakes God for human: "The LORD appeared to [Abraham] by the terebinths of Mamre; he was sitting at the entrance of the tent as the day grew hot. Looking up, he saw three men standing near him. As soon as he saw them, he ran from the entrance of the tent to greet them and, bowing to the ground, he said, 'My lords, if it please you, do not go on past your servant. Let a little water be brought; bathe your feet and recline under the tree'" (Gen. 18:1–4).

Although Jewish tradition understands the three men Abraham sees as angels, the first sentence tells us that it is God, not other divine beings, who appears to Abraham here. God appears in human drag, clothed so perfectly in human terms—flesh, bone, time, space, gender, and actual clothing—that Abraham, who recognized God from the moment God first spoke to him, thinks he is seeing men who, as his offers of hospitality make clear, have human feelings, frailties, and needs.[12] For most of my life, I thought that human terms were always imposed on God by human beings, and that God suffers them as a concession to human limitations. But in this scene, it is clear that as in the scene where Moses sees God's back, God chooses to present in human terms, because Abraham, from the first, has been ready and willing to relate to God without them.[13] God's appearance in human drag enables Abraham to interact with God with an intimacy and ease that would otherwise be impossible, as we see when Abraham offers God hospitality.

But as this scene suggests, when God presents completely in human terms, God cannot be recognized as God, just as I am usually not recognized as transgender when I present myself to strangers as a woman. God seems content to be seen as human by Abraham here, just as I am happy to have those I interact with in passing see me as a woman who was born and raised female. But if I want others to really know me, I need them to see me not as someone who fits binary definitions of female but as someone whose gender cannot be completely understood in binary terms. Similarly, as we see in this scene, in order for human beings to recognize God as God, God needs to appear in ways that do not completely fit human terms.

On the other hand, if God does not present in human terms at all, then most human beings find it hard to relate to God, as we see when, at the end of the giving of the Ten Commandments, the Israelites say to Moses, "You speak to us . . . and we will obey; but let not God speak to us, lest we die" (Exod. 20:16). Although the Torah portrays Abraham, Sarah, Moses, and others as having a greater tolerance for God's incomprehensibility than the Israelites do, even when relating to these intimates, God makes some concessions to human terms, appearing in particular times and places, and communicating in what the Torah describes as a voice that speaks in human language.

The balancing act God engages in when relating to human beings is familiar to many transgender people. If we fit ourselves too completely into binary gender terms, we find ourselves back in the closet, hidden from others the way God is hidden from Abraham by appearing as three men. If we present ourselves in ways that don't fit familiar terms at all, we, like God thundering at Sinai, risk being seen as incomprehensibly, dangerously other.

As this analogy suggests, even though God cannot be understood in human terms, in many ways, the relationships the Torah portrays between God and human beings are still human relationships, shaped, like relationships among human beings, by anxieties, misunderstandings, and the need for give-and-take. We see such give-and-take in Genesis 15, when, for the first time, Abraham responds to God's vague promises by demanding that God address Abraham's present-day concerns:

> Some time later, the word of the LORD came to Abram in a vision. [God] said: "Fear not, Abram, for I am a shield to you; your reward shall be very great." But Abram said, "O LORD God, what can You give me, seeing that I shall die childless, and the one in charge of my household is Dammesek Eliezer?" Abram said further, "Since you have granted me no offspring, my steward will be my heir." The word of the LORD came to him in reply, "That one shall not be your heir; none but your very own issue shall be your heir." [God] took him outside and said, "Look toward heaven and count the stars, if you are able to count them . . . So shall your offspring be." And because he put his trust in the LORD, [God] reckoned it to his merit. (Gen. 15:1–6)

This is the third time God has spoken to Abraham. As on previous occasions, God appears without warning and offers general assurances of future blessings. But the first two times, God does all the talking. Here, Abraham interrupts to insist that God address his very human anxieties, making it clear that he is concerned not with some unspecified future but with the practical, present-day problem of having no heir.

As a human being might, God responds by showing that God understands and plans to address Abraham's fear that his steward Eliezer will be his heir. But unlike a human being, God also responds by drastically changing the way in which God appears. God leaves the vision through which God has been communicating with Abraham and descends into human space and time, entering Abraham's tent, taking him outside, and looking up with him at the sky. Although God does not appear in bodily form, for a moment, God embraces Abraham's limited human point of view, gazing with him at the stars that God, like Abraham, sees as numberless points of light in a vast and distant heaven.[14]

Unlike God's "Where are you?" to Eve and Adam in the Garden, or my presentation of myself as a boy to Wendy, God's embrace of human terms here doesn't hide or misrepresent God's nature. Abraham knows that the God who takes him outside to look at the stars is the same God who spoke to him through the vision. God does not suffer or submit to being experienced by Abraham in terms of human time and space; it is God's idea to appear in these terms, and God clearly does so in order to help Abraham understand the future God is promising him. To Abraham, a childless old man who believes he is approaching the end of his life without an heir, the future that, to God, is already certain seems unimaginable. By entering human time and space and looking up with Abraham at what human beings see as heaven, God is able to give Abraham a concrete way—counting stars—to imagine the future God is promising him, for no matter how numerous they are, the counting of stars always begins with one, just as the people God already sees descending from Abraham will begin, for Abraham, with a single son.

In this dialogue, God is clearly and unabashedly God: inhuman, incorporeal, incomprehensible. When, at the end, God appears in human terms, it is not because, as Maimonides would say, the Torah is presenting God anthropomorphically, but because the Torah portrays God's relationship with Abraham as not only a divine but also a human relationship. That relationship is driven by God's divine plan to create a nation—that's why God speaks to Abraham—but as we see here, it is also shaped by Abraham's human needs and limitations. Even when the word of the Lord comes to Abraham through a vision, that word comes in language Abraham understands, in an encounter that unfolds, as human beings require, through a series of moments and events that can be remembered and transmitted to later generations as a human story about a God we cannot comprehend: a God who is not bound as we are by time or space, beginnings or ends, but who, from time to time, appears in ways we can understand, entering our tents and our lives, understanding our anxieties, answering our fears, and leading us out beyond our walls to look up at the stars.

"Shall Not the Judge of the Earth Deal Justly?"

Although God never spoke to me as God does to Abraham, never promised me blessings, demanded that I change my life, or invited me out to stargaze, I doubt I would have survived my childhood if I had not felt God's presence. But though I never doubted that God was there, my relationship with God was troubled. God, my creator and sustainer, had given me a body that didn't feel like mine. God was the reason I lived in fear and hiding, the reason I felt invisible and unloved. God was the source of the pain that came from the mismatch between my body and my soul, a pain that sometimes became so great that I was sure that either it would kill me or that I should kill myself. God alone knew how bad I felt, God alone was the source of my suffering, and God alone could save me by changing my body to fit my soul.

Night after night, I begged God to change my body; night after night, God did nothing but murmur, "I am here."

I didn't have the power to make God relieve my anguish, but though I didn't realize it then, I did have another power: the power to make sense of God's incomprehensible actions in human terms, to tell myself why God was making me suffer, to decide what my suffering meant about me and about God. Because I was a child, the sense I made was simple: either God was bad for hurting me, or God was hurting me because I was bad. I knew God wasn't bad, so, I decided, God must want me to suffer because I deserved to suffer. Because I had never done anything to deserve this suffering, I must be suffering because I was essentially, irredeemably, bad. God was not ignoring my pleas; God was passing judgment upon me.

Don't get me wrong: I never thought that God was punishing me for having a female gender identity, because I didn't believe that God would punish me for being what God had made me. But bad children, I knew, deserved to be punished, and because I was being punished, it must mean that to God, who knew me inside out, I was truly bad. I couldn't convince God to end my anguish, but I could turn my pain into a sign of God's presence and God's justice, so that whenever I was hurting, I interpreted it as God saying, "I am doing this to you, and you deserve it."

The terms I used were childish, but in trying to make sense of my suffering, I was exercising the kind of power Abraham exercises in his dialogue with God about the judgment of Sodom and Gomorrah—the power to define God's role in the human world:

Then the LORD said [to Abraham], "The outrage of Sodom and Gomorrah is so great, and their sin is so grave! I will go down to see whether they have acted altogether according to the outcry that has reached Me; if not, I will take note." Abraham came forward and said, "Will You sweep away the innocent along with the guilty? What if there should be fifty innocent within the city; will You then wipe out the place and not forgive it for the sake of the innocent fifty who are in it? Far be it from You to do such a thing, to bring death upon the innocent as well as the guilty, so that innocent and guilty fare alike. Far be it from You! Shall not the Judge of all the earth deal justly?" (Gen. 18:20–25)

Abraham, like me, assumes that even though God is responsible for human suffering, God's actions are not arbitrary, cruel, or incomprehensible (or, as I put it when I was a child, "bad"), that they make sense in terms of human morality. But unlike me, Abraham has a clear idea of God's role in the suffering God is about to cause: he sees God as the Judge of all the earth, and therefore bound, like human judges, to render judgments that human beings can recognize as just.

I never figured out exactly why I deserved my suffering, but Abraham defines specific standards for whether God's destruction of Sodom and Gomorrah can be considered just in human terms:[15]

And the LORD answered [Abraham], "If I find within the city of Sodom fifty innocent ones, I will forgive the whole place for their sake." Abraham spoke up, saying, "Here I venture to speak to my LORD, I who am but dust and ashes: What if the fifty innocent should lack five? Will You destroy the whole city for want of the five?" And [God] answered, "I will not destroy if I find forty-five there." But he spoke to [God] again, and said, "What if forty should be found there?" And [God] answered, "I will not do it, for the sake of the forty." And he said, "Let not my LORD be angry if I go on: What if thirty should be found there?" And [God] answered, "I will not do it if I find thirty there." And he said, "I venture again to speak to my LORD: What if twenty should be found there?" And [God] answered, "I will not destroy, for the sake of the twenty." And he said, "Let not my LORD be angry if I speak but this last time: What if ten should be found there?" And [God] answered, "I will not destroy, for the sake of the ten." When the LORD had finished speaking to Abraham, [God] departed; and Abraham returned to his place. (Gen. 18:26–33)

Unlike my attempts to intercede with God, in this dialogue, God responds to what Abraham says. But though God accepts Abraham's proposals, God doesn't tell Abraham any more than God told me about how God judges humanity. After raising the subject of Sodom and Gomorrah, God simply agrees to every standard of judgment Abraham proposes.[16] God never makes counterproposals, explains God's own standards of judgment, or even says whether God agrees with Abraham that God is obligated to act in ways that human beings will see as just. It is Abraham who dubs God "Judge of all the earth," defining God's role in terms that, according to Abraham, oblige God to meet human standards of justice. It is Abraham who sets the standards by which the destruction of Sodom and Gomorrah could be considered just, Abraham who keeps tightening those standards, and Abraham who ultimately decides that it is just to destroy the cities even if nine innocent people are swept away along with the guilty.[17]

Although Abraham does not assume that God's divine idea of justice will conform to human standards—if he did, he wouldn't keep proposing his own—he doesn't seem to notice that God never actually accepts either the role of Judge of all the earth or Abraham's claim that God shouldn't and wouldn't sweep away the innocent with the guilty.[18] Indeed, the Torah does not tell us whether God tries to determine how many innocent people live in Sodom and Gomorrah. The cities are destroyed after two angels visit Sodom, are assaulted by a mob, and lead Abraham's nephew Lot, Lot's wife, and their daughters to safety. As a result, it is not clear that Abraham's definition of doing justly had any more effect on God's judgment of Sodom and Gomorrah than my childhood pleas had on God's decision to leave me in a male body.

Like me, Abraham speaks to God from a position of powerlessness: not only does he know that he cannot control what God does, but he also fears that he is acting presumptuously and risking God's rage every time he proposes a new standard for God's judgment. But though neither of us had the power to change God's actions, both of us—Abraham, God's intimate, and me, a lonely, terrified child—had, and exercised, the power to define God in human terms. Abraham used that power to define God as Judge of all the earth; I used it to define God as the unyielding judge of me.

Whether or not God agreed with our definitions, God did not dispute them, and so we were free to believe them and live our lives accordingly. Indeed, God never speaks up for or against human definitions of God. As a result, all of us—whether we are saints or secularists, suffering children or religious extremists who murder in God's name—have the power to interpret God's actions, define God's role in the world and in our lives, and make sense of God in our own terms.

Those terms may not affect God's actions, but they can certainly affect our own. My decision that God had doomed me because I was bad led me both to passively accept my misery and to ignore my own moral responsibilities: I knew that no matter what I did, I would always be bad, and so I felt little motivation to live up to ideals of goodness. By contrast, Abraham's naming of God as Judge of all the earth drove Abraham to propose stricter and stricter standards for God's judgment, despite his fear that he was making God angry.

Abraham doesn't risk God's wrath out of affection for Sodom and Gomorrah (his assumption that God is going to destroy the cities suggests that he too has heard the outcry against them) or even out of concern for his cousin Lot, who would not necessarily be protected by God's agreement to spare the cities if ten innocents were found there. Rather, Abraham defines God as a Judge he expects to deal justly because that is the meaning he wants to find in God's actions. As one of Abraham's descendants, Dr. Martin Luther King Jr., might have said, Abraham bends the arc of God's relationship with humanity toward justice, prompting us to judge God by human standards of justice, to see God's presence as manifested through justice, and, by implication, to see injustice as hiding or driving God away.

Although the Torah makes it clear that God destroys Sodom and Gomorrah as punishment for the communal brutality we see in the story of the angels' visit, some religious traditions interpret God as condemning the cities for what came to be called sodomy—sex between men. These traditions define God in terms of homicidal homophobia, prompting us to see God's presence not in justice but in the murder of gay people and in the destruction of those who accept them. I never read the Torah that way, but as a child, I too perverted the human power to define God: I saw God as a Judge whose idea of justice included torturing a child and projected onto God my own childish morality, imagining that God, like me, sees everyone as essentially, unalterably good or bad, no matter what we do or how we grow and change.

Few of us have had Abraham's experience of hearing God agreeing to our standards for divine justice. Whether we name God judge or torturer, healer or hater, punisher or protector, God usually responds with silence. That silence can be maddening, heartbreaking, enraging; it may lead us to feel that God is not there at all. But God's silence gives each of us the power—the awful power—to define God's role in our lives and in the world in ways that, whether or not they affect God's actions, can profoundly shape our own.

God's Identity

I never discussed the Torah with my father, but if we had talked about the judgment of Sodom and Gomorrah, I suspect he would have considered Abraham defining God as Judge of all the earth a perfect example of human beings creating God in our own image. My father would be right that Abraham's naming of God reflects Abraham's wishes, hopes, and values. But though God accepts Abraham's standards for deciding whether the cities should be destroyed, the Torah makes it clear that God is not defined by Abraham's terms. Just before their dialogue, God appears in a form—three men—that Abraham doesn't recognize. A few chapters later, the God who, according to Abraham, would never sweep away the innocent with the guilty orders Abraham, for no reason at all, to sacrifice Isaac, the miraculously conceived son on whom God's promises of future blessings depend. Because God does not act or appear in ways that make sense in human terms, God does not have what human beings call an identity. God is what God is and will be what God will be, no matter what we say or wish, believe or hope, remember or expect.

God's lack of an identity that would help human beings recognize God from one appearance to another and predict how God will act may not matter to Abraham, Maimonides, and other spiritually exalted souls. But most of us find it hard to relate to those who don't have identities that enable us to recognize them as the people we have known in the past and assure that they will be the same people in the future. That was what upset my son most about my transition: not that I was presenting myself as a woman (he went to a school that was so gender progressive it had official cross-dressing days), but that my change in appearance and behavior might mean that he could no longer count on me to be the father he loved.

I understand how he felt. Binary gender identities are promises that we have always been, and will always be, the males or females we seem to be. Although my son didn't realize it, before my transition, I broke gender's promise of identity every time I presented myself as a man, because I knew that who I was to myself was not who I was pretending to be. Once I began living as myself, I broke the promise of identity in a different way, by making it clear that I was not the man my son and others had believed I was and counted on me to be. No matter how many times I told my son that I was the same parent who had loved him even before he was born and would love him until my dying day, my gender transition told him the opposite: that he could not count on me to be the person I seemed to be.

Of course, it is not only transgender people who break the promise of identity; we all do. No matter what identities we present, no matter how committed we are to remaining the same people we have been, human beings change: sometimes because we want to; sometimes because we have to; sometimes in ways, like growing older, that everyone expects; sometimes in ways that, like a sudden disability or religious conversion, astonish even ourselves. In fact, it is because human beings change that we assign identities to our children as soon as they are born. We know that infants look and act completely different within days of their birth and will continue to change throughout their lives, and so we give them names to identify them as the same people they were when they first drew breath. Gender, the other identity we assign at birth, has the same purpose. By identifying infants in terms of male or female genitals, we tell ourselves that they will remain the same males or females from birth to death.

As we see in God's encounters with Abraham, God has an extreme version of the identity problems my son has with me. God's ways of presenting to human beings vary drastically from situation to situation, person to person, and even from moment to moment, as when God shifts from presenting as a voice in a vision to leading Abraham out to look at the stars. Human identities tell others a lot about who we are, who we have been, and who we intend to be.[19] But God's appearances in the Torah are not expressions of identity. These appearances don't tell us who or what God is to Godself—that, as Maimonides says, is unknowable, beyond human understanding or experience. Similarly, the way God appears at any given moment says nothing about how God has appeared in the past or how God will appear in the future.

Other Iron Age deities were identified with specific images, manifestations, and phenomena, such as thunder, fertility, or war. The God portrayed in the Torah rejects all those forms of identity. God is invisible and formless, and God appears in so many different ways that it is impossible to identify God with any of them, as the Torah emphasizes in this famous scene from the life of the prophet Elijah: "And lo, the LORD passed by. There was a great and mighty wind, splitting mountains and shattering rocks by the power of the LORD; but the LORD was not in the wind. After the wind, an earthquake. After the earthquake—fire; but the LORD was not in the fire. And after the fire—a still, small voice. When Elijah heard it, he wrapped his mantle about his face and went out and stood at the entrance of the cave" (I Kings 19:11–13).

The Torah makes it clear that though God causes the wind, earthquake, and fire, they do not represent God: God is not "in" them. It is not until Elijah hears the still, small voice that Elijah believes that God has finally appeared. (The Torah neither confirms nor denies Elijah's belief, withholding comment on whether God is "in" the still, small voice.)

But as Elijah no doubt knows, even if God appears here as a still, small voice, it does not mean that we can identify God with still, small voices, because God may never appear that way again. In fact, in God's most famous public appearance—the giving of the Ten Commandments at Mount Sinai—God's voice is neither still nor small: "Now Mount Sinai was all in smoke, for the LORD had come down upon it in fire; the smoke rose like the smoke of a kiln, and the whole mountain trembled violently. The blare of the horn grew louder and louder. As Moses spoke, God answered him in thunder" (Exod. 19:18–19).

As in God's appearance to Elijah (and unlike God's appearances to Abraham, Sarah, Hagar, Isaac, and Jacob), God's appearance on Mount Sinai is accompanied by spectacular disruptions of nature: fire descending, smoke rising, the mountain shaking. Here, God does seem to be "in" the fire (God "come[s] down . . . in fire" [Exod. 19:18]), and when God speaks, God does so not in a still, small voice, but in thunder.

Even though Moses has told the assembled Israelites that the fire, smoke, shaking, and thunder on Mount Sinai are signs that God, as promised, is appearing to them (Exod. 19:11), the Israelites can't tell which, if any, of these manifestations of divine power represent the appearance of God. In fact, according to one rabbinic story, God appeared to the Israelites in completely different guises at Sinai and during their exodus through the heaped-up waters of the sea: "At the sea [God] appeared to them as a mighty hero doing battle . . . At Sinai [God] appeared to them as an old man full of mercy."[20] That is why, this text goes on to say, God introduces the giving of the Ten Commandments with a self-identification—"I am the LORD your God who brought you out of the land of Egypt" (Exod. 20:2). God wants to ensure that the Israelites know that the "I am" they hear at Sinai refers to the same God they have experienced before and will experience in the future: "'I am the LORD thy God' [means] I am [God] who was in Egypt, and I am [God] who was at the sea. I am [God] who was in the past and I am [God] who will be in the future. I am [God] who is in this world and I am [God] who will be in the world to come."[21] This account emphasizes that without God's self-identifying "I am," the Israelites would have no way of knowing that the same God who split the sea is thundering commandments from Mount Sinai, because God appears in such different ways at different times.

But even without this rabbinic elaboration, it is clear from the declaration "I am the LORD your God who brought you out of the land of Egypt" that God believes the Israelites need a verbal declaration of identity in order to recognize the voice speaking to them out of the smoke and fire as the voice of *their* God, the same God who delivered them from slavery. God's "I am" is more effective than the fire, smoke, shaking, and thunder in identifying God for one of the very reasons that Maimonides says human language always misrepresents God: because language implies similarity, in this case the similarity—the identity—of the God speaking at Sinai to the God who brought the Israelites out of Egypt.

The commandments that follow God's "I am" make it clear that God is willing not only to self-identify but also to be identified in human terms. Although God forbids the Israelites from making any visual representations of the Divine (Exod. 20:4), God does not prohibit them from representing God in words or stories, because both God and the Israelites need human language to establish God's identity across time, space, and innumerable variations in individual experiences of the Divine.[22] As God acknowledges at Sinai, our relationships with God, like other long-term human relationships, are more than just our present-tense experience of God at any given moment. They are historical, stories we tell ourselves and others that enable us to recognize God across lives, generations, and millennia.

Of course, as Maimonides explains, human language cannot help but misrepresent God.[23] That is true even when God is doing the talking. By saying "I," God implies that God is a subject, an "I," in the same way human speakers are, and that God, like a human speaker, can be defined in terms of predicates, characteristics—such as God's deliverance of the Israelites from Egypt—that are separate from God's essence. As Maimonides shows, these implications betray God's uniqueness and oneness.

This kind of compromise—using language that misrepresents us to communicate identities that others can understand—is familiar to many transgender people. Indeed, the word "transgender" itself makes this sort of compromise. When I identify myself as a woman, I am telling others how I see myself, how I want them to see me, how I live and how I plan to live for the rest of my life. When I identify myself as a transsexual, I am telling others that my sense of who I am does not match my physical sex or the gender I was assigned at birth. But when I say that I am transgender, all I am saying is that my gender is more complicated than simply male or female. Like God's "I am" at Sinai, when I identify myself as transgender, I am accepting being misrepresented as an individual in exchange for an identity that has social, historical, and political meaning to others.[24]

This trade-off—that we can only affirm our identities by using language that misrepresents our individuality—applies not just to God and to trans-gender people but to everyone. As Maimonides points out, because human terms imply similarity, the language we use to identify ourselves always overemphasizes our similarities with others and with past and present versions of ourselves, and obscures our changeableness and individuality.

The queerer we are, the less we fit established terms and categories, the more the language we use to identify ourselves will misrepresent us. That was why I didn't come out to Wendy—because I knew that the language we shared could not tell her who and what I was. But, as I learned after my transition, and as God shows at Sinai, we can use terms that misrepresent us to identify ourselves in ways that, however imperfectly, reveal us to others and authentically express our relationships to them. When I tell my son, "I will always be your father," the terms I use misrepresent me by ignoring my gender identification and transition, but they truthfully express who I am in relation to him. No matter what else I am, I will always be the person who fathered my son, and I will always be committed to being his father. Similarly, no matter what else God is, God will always be the God who led the Israelites out of bondage, and, as God declares at Sinai, is committed to being their God.

I don't know how God feels about the trade-offs required to identify ourselves in these terms, but I know that when it comes to people I love, what matters most is not who I am to myself, but who I am to them. That doesn't mean that I could continue living as a man for my son's sake, any more than God could consent to the Israelites' desire to relate to God through idols and images: both of us have to be true to the ways we are incomprehensible to others, even to those we love. But like God at Sinai, I can, and do, accept being identified in terms that misrepresent me for the sake of relationships with those who, without those terms, couldn't identify me at all.

"I Am What I Will Be"

The Torah rarely gives us any indication of why God chooses to be iden-tified in one way or another. But there is one scene in which we see God wrestling with this question: the scene at the burning bush in which Moses asks how he should identify God to the enslaved Israelites whom God wants him to lead out of Egypt: "When I come to the Israelites and say to them, 'The God of your fathers has sent me to you,' and they ask me, 'What is [God's] name?' what shall I say to them?" (Exod. 3:13).

Moses doesn't question God's ability to bring the Israelites out of Egypt, but he has grave doubts that the Israelites will recognize a nameless, invisible God who has not been much in evidence over the past four centuries of slavery and who, unlike the deities of Egypt, has no temples, rites, priesthood, or religion. Moses is asking God for a name that will show the Israelites that Moses, an octogenarian exile who hasn't been in Egypt since he was young man, really does have a special relationship with God, and will also help the Israelites make sense of who God is to them.

I don't know what I would have said if my son had asked me, as Moses asks God, how he should name me to others. He never stopped calling me "Daddy," naming me as the man he wants me, always, to be. That name expresses his relationship with me, but when he calls me "Daddy," people who don't know us look at us uncomprehendingly, wondering whether my son has misspoken or they have misheard. My son never came up with a name for me that expresses who I am to him in a way that makes sense to others.

I don't blame him. I found it almost impossible to name myself. I had always hated the male name, "Jay," that I was given at birth, and when I began the process of gender transition, I was eager to find a new name that would express who I truly am. But because I had never lived as myself, I didn't yet know the self I was trying to identify. I latched onto a generically feminine name, one that had little to do with me other than signifying a female gender identity. Even people who were supportive of my transition thought that name was utterly wrong for me—so wrong that my friends begged me to choose another. A male friend offered me a name he had always loved. I loved it, too—it sounded mysterious, alluring, and glamorous, as though I were a *femme fatale* in a movie. But because I wasn't any of those things, it soon became clear that that name, too, wasn't mine.

After months of patiently calling me names that didn't fit me, my friend Annie told me that I needed to find a name that expressed who I was in way that would make sense to others. I agreed, but I couldn't imagine what that name might be. Moses at the burning bush wonders how to identify a God the enslaved Israelites have never experienced. I wondered what name could identify a self I was still in the process of becoming.

"How about Joy?" Annie suggested. I had considered "Joy," because it was the closest female name to "Jay." But as a way of naming *me*, it seemed ridiculous, because, as I told Annie, at that point in my transition, I was the most miserable person I knew. Annie insisted: "It fits how I see you changing," she said. "You aren't becoming a different person—just opening up in the middle." Suddenly, the name made sense to me, not as an expression of who I was, but as a mission statement: "Joy" named why I was becoming myself—to feel joy and to bring joy—in terms that even those who could not understand transgender identity could understand. "Joy" was the right name for me, because, as Annie said, it signified the process of my becoming.

At the burning bush, God also seems to have difficulty settling on a name:

> Moses said to God, "When I come to the Israelites and say to them, 'The God of your fathers has sent me to you,' and they ask me, 'What is [God's] name?' what shall I say to them?" And God said to Moses, "Ehyeh-Asher-Ehyeh." [God] continued, "Thus shall you say to the Israelites, 'Ehyeh sent me to you.'" And God said further to Moses, "Thus shall you speak to the Israelites: The LORD, the God of your fathers, the God of Abraham, the God of Isaac, and the God of Jacob, has sent me to you:
>
> This shall be My name forever,
> This My appellation for all eternity." (Exod. 3:13–15)

Like me, God embraces two different names, "Ehyeh-Asher-Ehyeh" and "Ehyeh," before settling on a third: "The LORD [YHVH], the God of your fathers, God of Abraham, God of Isaac, and God of Jacob." The name God finally embraces combines several different forms of identification. First, it identifies God through the famous tetragrammaton, the Hebrew letters *yud hay vav hay* (transliterated in English as "YHVH," and translated above as "the LORD"), a word that might be a verb, a noun, or both, and is incomprehensible because it refers to nothing other than God.[25] After expressing God's incomprehensibility, this formulation goes on to identify God in terms of God's relationships with the patriarchs from whom the Israelites are descended. As I tried to do when assuring my son that I would always be his father, God gives Moses a name that assures the Israelites that although they cannot understand who or what God is, God will always be the God they (or rather, their ancestors) knew in the past.

But before settling on this formulation, God, as though thinking out loud, offers two versions of a name, "Ehyeh-Asher-Ehyeh," that identifies God not with God's incomprehensibility or God's past relationships, but in terms of something God and human beings have in common: the process of becoming. Ehyeh-Asher-Ehyeh can be translated "I am that I am," "I will be what I will be," or "I am what I will be."[26] (The shortened version, Ehyeh, can be understood either as "I am" or "I will be.") These translations sound different, but in effect they name God in the same way. When we say that God is what God is, we acknowledge that the way God appears at any given moment does not express, define, or limit God. Because God is what God is, God will be whatever God will be, appearing as a voice from a bush that burns but is not consumed, as three men with dusty feet, as the revolutionary who upends the theocracy of Egypt and as the conservative who establishes a new theocracy in Israel, as a deliverer of Egyptian slaves and murderer of Egyptians' firstborn children, to name just a few of God's manifestations.[27] However God appears in the present and has appeared in the past, we cannot know how God will appear in the future. God is not only what we know God is: God is also what God will be.

If there had been a female name that meant "I am what I will be," I would have embraced it during transition. I was no longer the man I had been, and wasn't yet the person I was growing into: I defined myself in terms of what I was becoming. I still do. As other trans people warned me before I started to live as myself, the process of transition is never complete. I will never just be what I am; I will always be what I will be.

That is what upset my son. Once I had broken gender's promise of identity, he knew that whatever I was at any given moment, I would be what I would be. But transgender people do not have a monopoly on becoming. All human beings change. Transgender or not, we are never just what we are at any given moment. Our bodies change, our relationships change, our lives change, and so do the ways we present and identify ourselves. We are trajectories, potentials, ongoing revelations of selves that are always unfolding.

The name "Ehyeh-Asher-Ehyeh" invites us to see that we, however distantly, share in God's indefinability, because we, like God, are not limited to or determined by the terms by which we identify ourselves. However passionately or desperately we insist that what we are what we are, like the God in whose image we are created, we are what we will be.

FOUR

READING BETWEEN THE BINARIES

A Leaf on the Tree of Life

From the moment I started reading it to relieve my boredom in synagogue, I heard the Torah speaking to my life as a trans child.

The narrating voice of the Torah was strangely familiar: cold, distant, occasionally tender, brutally direct about the potential for violence that I, living in terror and hiding, felt lurking in every relationship and situation. Like Adam and Eve, driven out from the Garden God had designed for them, I feared I would be driven from my home if my parents ever guessed I was not the boy they thought I was. Like Cain and Abel and Joseph and his brothers, I knew that family ties can bring rage as well as love. Like Jacob, I knew I was stealing my parents' blessings by impersonating the boy they meant to give them to, and I feared the curses I was certain would follow if those who cared for me glimpsed who I really was.

It was not only the stories the Torah told, but also the way the Torah told them, that spoke to the life I was living. The Torah's colorless, sketch-like narration; the lack of description of landscapes, scenes, clothing, interiors, figures, faces, sounds, or colors; the almost complete failure to acknowledge the feelings of the people the Torah portrayed, echoed my own dissociated relation to the world around me. My body tasted, felt, and perceived, but my real self, the self I felt I was, had no body. It—I—was buried in the boy who played and learned and grew, a shadow self whose world was a shadow of the world my body experienced. My real self, the self I felt I was, had no relationships, no opportunities to see or hear or taste or feel. The Torah's depictions of human lives, in which even the most shocking events, like Cain's murder of Abel, begin and end in a few brief words, felt oddly akin to my shadow life, in which years passed like days, intimates were as distant as strangers, and whatever happened among them happened far away.

My childish, self-centered relationship with the Torah led me to focus on the parts that interested me and ignore what didn't: genealogical lists, instructions about constructing the Tabernacle and performing sacrifices, and laws that I didn't feel, or didn't want to feel, applied to me. My sense that I had a right to ignore the Torah's laws seemed to me to be confirmed by the fact that so many of them were framed in terms of binary gender. It was easy to tell myself that laws that assumed that everyone was simply male or female didn't apply to me.

In this perverse sense, I felt liberated by the Torah's reliance on binary gender, as though it was giving me permission not to judge myself according to its laws, or amputate myself to fit them. But, as the poet W. H. Auden said, "To be free is often to be lonely."[1] The freedom I felt to read the Torah as though it were speaking to me alone reflected the fact that though I saw myself as Jewish, I didn't feel like part of the Jewish people, because I was sure no Jewish community, past or present, would accept me if they knew I wasn't the boy I appeared to be. The absolute rejection I imagined made it easy to tell myself that laws that had bound Jews together for millennia had no claim on me.

I didn't understand my strange relationship to Judaism until a few years ago, when, after hearing about my childhood, Rabbi Jill Hammer told me that I was a "feral Jew," a Jew whose sense of Jewishness was developed in isolation. My isolation was forced on me by growing up in a world that had no place for transgender people, but it freed me to create a private Judaism tailored to my particular needs. As a feral Jew, I invented my own readings of the Torah (some would say, my own Torah); my own selective Jewish tradition; my own religious practice, a private hodgepodge drawn from Orthodox and non-Orthodox customs; and my own prayers. I even had my own private covenant with God. My covenant was not based on God's promise to Abraham, or the Exodus from Egypt, or the giving of the Ten Commandments at Sinai. It was based on the solidarity I imagined God and I shared as invisible, incomprehensible strangers dwelling in the midst of those who, unlike us, had bodies and lives that fit human categories. God alone saw me as I truly was, so I knew from an early age that I had to bear witness to God.

But though I felt free to pick and choose among the Torah's laws, there was one I could neither ignore nor obey: "A woman must not put on man's apparel, nor shall a man wear women's clothing; for whoever does these things is abhorrent to the LORD your God" (Deut. 22:5).[2] When I read this verse I always flinched, as though Moses for a moment had turned away from the Israelites he was exhorting to aim his ferociously binary gaze at me.

I know now that there are good reasons to think that Moses was not, in fact, speaking to people like me, that this law was aimed not at prohibiting what we would now call expression of transgender identity, but, as Rashi and other commentators suggest, at prohibiting cross-dressing for fraudulent, idolatrous, or sexual purposes.[3] However, the Torah doesn't say that, and because the Moses we hear in Deuteronomy is so passionately attached to binary thinking in terms of both morality and gender, I never doubted that he was talking to me. Moses, who knew God more intimately than I ever will, wanted me to know that the God I loved "abhorred" me—abhorred not the behavior prohibited by the law, but me, me as I knew myself, the real me who could only be visible, present, and fully alive when I lived my female gender identity by doing what Moses calls "putting women's clothing on a man's body."

As a child who cross-dressed rarely and in terror, I found it easy to believe that God found me abhorrent. After all, I was living in hiding because I assumed that if I didn't—if I expressed my female gender identity—everyone, even my own parents, would abhor me, because I, the real me, was abhorrent. I was so sure that I was abhorrent that I found Moses's declaration strangely reassuring. No matter how abhorrent I was, Moses seemed to be saying, God would always be there with me, paying attention to the smallest details of my existence, down to the scraps of cloth I wore.

Abused children learn to associate pain with intimacy, rejection with love. That was how I understood what Moses was telling me about my relationship with God. God was there, watching me get dressed, abhorring me morning and night, because God truly cared about me. I assumed that my parents only loved me and tolerated my presence because they couldn't see who I really was, which meant they didn't really love me at all. According to Moses, God abhorred me because God *did* see me, but unlike what I assumed about my parents, God would never turn me away.

No matter how abhorrent I was, God would always be there, a combination of intimacy and rejection that I mistook for love.

I am no longer a child living in hiding; I no longer confuse abhorrence with love. And I know now that what Moses says in this verse does not describe God's relationship with me, that Moses's insistence that God "abhors" people who cross-dress has everything to do with Moses, and nothing to do with God. I can't tell if Moses here is voicing his personal version of what we now call transphobia, or if he is mistaking the transphobia built into his Iron Age culture for transphobia on the part of God. But whatever the source of Moses's feelings, the Torah makes it clear that in this verse, it is Moses rather than God who is speaking. When I read this as Moses's voice, I realize how different this passage is from laws the Torah portrays as being given directly by God. For example, God prohibits murder without saying that God abhors the people who commit it. And even when I childishly assumed that Moses was right about how God felt about me, I never actually felt God's abhorrence. God surrounded me and held me, listened to my pleas and prayers, kept me alive in the depths of despair. Even when I found it hard to feel anything but fear, self-hatred, and pain, God's presence felt like love.

I have changed a lot since I first heard the Torah speak to me. Now that I am living as myself, the world has become brighter and darker, more dangerous and more generous, brimming with emotions and sensations I used to perceive dimly, like a ghost moving through mist. I can see now how much of human experience is stripped away in the Torah's narration, how little it says about what the few human beings it portrays felt or saw, feared or tasted, did or desired.

In the Torah's storytelling, the blare of human experience is muted, so that we, like Eve and Adam in the Garden, can hear God moving among leaves and lives. With Abraham, we hear God speaking to us from beyond; with Sarah, we discover that God is close enough to notice us when, in our hearts, we laugh. As we read the Torah, we, like God, watch generations bloom and fade from one sentence to the next, and see entire lives reduced to a few brief strokes: Cain arranging his sacrifice on his altar; Hagar laying her dying son under a bush. They cannot see us, but we, like God, are there. Like God, we know the larger stories that, to them, have not yet begun to unfold. In what to them are the most difficult moments of their lives, we recognize, as God does, the seeds of a future that has nothing, and everything, to do with them.

Now that I no longer live in a state of dissociation, I don't read the Torah's stripped-down style as reflecting my personal distance from life; instead, I recognize it as telling stories in such a way that the busy richness of being human cannot distract us from God's presence, so that we can see the intersection of human concerns, like Abraham's anxiety about an heir, with divine concerns that stretch over centuries.[4] But though I read the Torah differently than I did when I was a child, I still hear it speaking to me as a transgender person, because the Torah speaks to my life as a Jew and a human being, and being transgender plays an important role in both. As I said at the beginning of this book, Jewish tradition describes the Torah as a tree of life—not as a tree of some lives, or as a tree of certain aspects of our lives, or as a tree of lives that fit binary gender categories, but as a tree of life itself, supporting, connecting, and sustaining the lives of all who cling to it. No matter how our identities, cultures, and religious practices may change over the millennia, this image of the Torah assures us that our lives grow out of the same trunk, the same roots.

In this sense, the idea that the Torah speaks to transgender lives is deeply traditional. I spent most of my life believing that I would be exiled from Jewish community—from every community—if I revealed my trans identity, but from my earliest childhood, that very community taught me that the Torah is a tree of life that includes my life, a leaf among its leaves.

Remove Them from the Camp

Because I have always read the Torah as speaking to my life as a transgender person, I haven't spent much time wondering whether, and how, the Torah might speak to the lives of trans people who, unlike me, don't assume that the Torah speaks to them.[5]

When transgender people read the Torah, we cannot help but notice that the Torah assumes that human beings are only and always either male or female. Not only doesn't the Torah mention people who identify as what we would now call transgender, it doesn't acknowledge gender identity—a personal sense of gender that might be different from one's physical sex—at all. Even the prohibition against cross-dressing assumes that no matter what men or women wear, they remain the gender they were assigned at birth. In the Torah, people who don't fit binary gender categories are not just invisible; we are unimaginable.

Maimonides emphasizes that because the Torah speaks in "the language of . . . men," it speaks in human language that reflects human assumptions.[6] Maimonides uses "the language of men" in the universal sense, but as many feminist critics have shown, the Torah is literally written in the language of *men*, in language that reflects a patriarchal version of the gender binary and assumes not only that human beings are always and only male or female, but also that women are subordinate to men.[7]

The Torah has been understood by many religious traditions to mean that God not only shares but also decrees the assumptions about gender built into its language. That language certainly makes it hard to distinguish human ideas about gender from God's ideas about what human beings are and should be.[8] But as Maimonides reminds us, God's absolute difference from humanity should make us doubt that God sees, understands, or values anything the same way human beings do. There is no reason to think that a God who is so utterly different from humanity is eternally invested in the Iron Age patriarchy we see in the Torah, when even human beings know that gender changes over time and varies from community to community.

Like feminists, trans people are free to read the Torah in ways that ignore or reject the ideas of gender built into its language. But I don't want a Torah that will only speak to me when I force it to. If I am going to root my life in the Torah, I want it to speak directly to my concerns as a transgender person. How can the Torah do that when it is written in the gender-binary-drenched language of Iron Age men?

To explore that question, let's examine one of the most binary sections of the Torah: the commandments regarding one of the many censuses that give the book of Numbers its English name:[9]

And the LORD spoke to Moses in the wilderness of Sinai, saying, "Record the Levites by [paternal] ancestral house and by clan:

record every male among them from the age of one month up." So
Moses recorded them at the command of the LORD, as he was bid-
den. These were the sons of Levi by name: Gershon, Kohath, and
Merari. These were the names of the sons of Gershon by clan: Libni
and Shimei . . . (Num. 3:14–18)

To Gershon belonged the clan of the Libnites, and the clan of the
Shimites: these were the clans of the Gershonites. The recorded en-
tries of all their males from the age of one month up, as recorded,
came to 7,500. The clans of the Gershonites were to camp behind
the Tabernacle, to the west. The chieftain of the ancestral house
of the Gershonites was Eliasaph the son of Lael. The duties of the
Gershonites in the Tent of Meeting comprised: the Tabernacle, the
tent, its covering, and the screen for the entrance of the Tent of
Meeting; the hangings of the enclosure; the screen for the entrance of the enclosure which surrounds the Tabernacle, the cords
thereof, and the altar—all the service connected with these.
(Num. 3:21–26)

In these commandments, the gender binary is not just assumed; it is the
basis for defining the sacred roles and responsibilities of the priestly tribe
of the Levites. According to this passage, Levites were first to be identified
by sex, and then, if male, recorded as a member of one of the three clans
founded by Levi's sons, Gershon, Kohath, and Merari, into which they
had been born.[10]

For Levite males, biology literally was destiny. As we see in the commandments regarding the Gershonites, each clan was assigned different
roles in terms of caring for "the Tent of Meeting," so when an infant Levite
was identified as male, he was assigned the sacred duties that would define
his adult life. If a baby was a Gershonite, for example, when the midwives
who delivered him declared, "It's a boy," they were also declaring that that
boy would grow up to take care of "the Tabernacle, the tent, its covering,
and the screen for the entrance of the Tent of Meeting; the hangings of the
enclosure; the screen for the entrance of the enclosure which surrounds
the Tabernacle, the cords thereof, and the altar" and other Gershonite
duties (Num. 3:25–26).

Although the Levite census commandments are only addressed to males, as feminist critics such as Cynthia Ozick have taught us to recognize, the gender binary assumptions built into the Torah's language of men mean that commandments that define male roles also define female roles.[11] Because the gender binary defines male and female in relation to one another, commandments to count males and assign identities and ritual roles based on their male ancestors are also commandments *not* to count females or consider how identity and role might be defined by mothers or maternal ancestors. Privilege, status, recognition, ritual role—whatever this commandment assigns to males, it implicitly denies to females. Male children swell the count of the tribe of Levi, so female children do not; males are assigned roles in taking care of the Tabernacle, so women are not; men define the identities of their offspring, so women do not. That is the power of gender binary assumptions: these commandments don't have to mention females or women in order to make clear the ways in which they do not count.[12]

In terms of the Levite census, women are insignificant, literally not worth counting, but trans people are less than insignificant: people who are not either and always male or female do not exist.[13] In these commandments, there is no gender apart from sex. Gender is defined by how others see our bodies, not by how we see ourselves. Levites who are seen and recorded as male will always be considered male, no matter how they understand or express themselves; Levites who are not recorded will always be female; and no Levites will ever be anything other than male or female.

But the very aspects of the Levite census commandments that erase the possibility of transgender people speak to my concerns as a transgender person, because they highlight the way binary gender, now as then, defines which of us do and do not count. For example, though the U.S. census, unlike the Levite census, counts both males and females, like the Levite census, the U.S. census counts males and females on the basis of physical sex, as the government's website explains: "For the purpose of Census Bureau surveys and the decennial census, sex refers to a person's biological sex."[14] Like the Levite census, the U.S. census treats maleness and femaleness as unchanging characteristics determined at birth. And like the Levite census, the U.S. census does not recognize anyone who isn't simply male or female.

Intersex and transgender people who are unwilling to identify ourselves in binary terms are not counted at all. Because there is no census data on trans people, no one knows the answers to crucial questions about us, such as how many of us are married or divorced or have children, or what our graduation or unemployment or homeless rates are. For purposes of public policy, health studies, tracking employment and housing discrimination, and any other decisions informed by census data, transgender Americans literally do not count.

Unlike the Levite census, in which gender was assigned by the census takers, the U.S. census allows for self-reporting. That enables transgender or intersex people who, like me, identify as either male or female to list ourselves according to our gender identities rather than our bodies. But when I identify myself as female on the U.S. census, I know that though I am telling the truth about my gender identity, I am not actually answering the question about biological sex. I have to either answer a question the census isn't asking or count myself out of the U.S. population.

Even though both the U.S. census and the Levite census assume that everyone is either and always male or female, the Levite census speaks to a crucial, and, for transgender people, often heartbreaking aspect of gender that the U.S. census does not: the way the gender binary defines us in relation to our families and our communities. The Levite census identifies individuals not only by their genitalia but also by their male relatives. To be counted in the census, one first had to be identified as an Israelite, a descendant of Abraham, Isaac, and Jacob, and then as a Levite, as a descendant of Jacob's son Levi, and then, through their male ancestors, as a descendant of one of Levi's sons, Gershon, Kohath, or Merari.

Most Americans do not identify themselves by patrilineal tribes and clans. But even in families where sons are no longer expected to be like their fathers and daughters are no longer expected to be like their mothers, relationships and identities are defined in language that, like the language of the Torah, is based on binary gender: spouses are either husbands or wives; parents are either mothers or fathers; children are either sons or daughters; siblings are either sisters or brothers. We still don't have a generally agreed-upon language for transgender family members; as in the days of the Levite census, the binary-based formulas for family relationships, expectations, roles, and duties do not include people who are not simply male or female.

Because our language for family relationships is based on binary gender, even in families where transgender members are embraced and loved, our transgender identities do not connect us to others the way identities based on being male or female, such as "mother" and "father," do. For example, from the time my son was born until my gender transition, people would talk about the ways in which he was like me, and he would look to me as a role model, an example of manhood that could help him understand who he was and what he could be. But since I began living as myself—since I became a father who lives as a woman—neither he nor anyone else tries to understand him (or, for that matter, my other children) in relation to me.

The Levite census commandments highlight the binding power of the gender binary, the way it connects individuals to family members and others through relationships, roles, and expectations that our culture, like that of the Israelites in the desert, base on binary gender—and so they speak, backhandedly, to the ways in which gender binary connections leave out people like me.

But these commandments speak directly to something that concerns many transgender people: the expectations that settle upon us when we are assigned to a gender, as the responsibilities of caring for parts of the Tabernacle settled upon Levite infants who were recorded as male. I am sure there were Gershonite men who delighted in caring for the Tabernacle, the tent, its covering, the screen for the entrance of the Tent of Meeting, and so on, just as many people today find meaning and joy in striving to be what they are told sons and daughters, mothers and fathers, men and women are supposed to be. But I am also sure that some Gershonite men did not delight in the tasks they had been assigned along with their maleness. Some of them must have struggled to fulfill those tasks, or disliked them, or felt crushed, rather than exalted, by them. I am certain about this, because the Gershonites' tasks were assigned when they were as young as one month old, without regard to their desires or abilities, or to the way their feelings or situations might change over their lives.

In some ways, the version of the gender binary into which I was born in the 1960s was a lot like the one we see in the Levite census commandments.

Like the Levite males, I was "recorded" as male on the basis of my infant genitalia, and, like them, I was supposed to live my entire life as the male I was determined to be. And though Americans think about gender in very different ways than they did when I was born (I'm not sure my parents then even knew the word "gender"), every child is still recorded at birth as male or female, and the first question we ask about an infant is still "Is it a boy or a girl?," because the answer still tells us so much—much too much—about the expectations, responsibilities, privileges, and prejudices gender will bring that child.

The Levite census commandments speak to the freight of expectations assigned along with binary gender—expectations by which I, like many transgender people, often feel crushed. Now that I'm living as myself, those expectations have shifted—people expect me to look and act like a woman instead of a man—but I am still constantly being judged according to the standards of binary gender.

Whether or not we are transgender, we are all subjected to what trans people call "gender surveillance," scrutinized to determine whether we are male or female. As I am reminded every time I enter a women's restroom, the more gender matters in a given situation, the more intense gender surveillance is, and the more intensely others react if they decide we do not look or act like the men or women they expect us to be.[15]

Moses's declaration that "a woman must not put on man's apparel, nor shall a man wear women's clothing" speaks directly to the importance we place on gender surveillance. Moses turns gender surveillance into a religious obligation, commanding Israelites to monitor themselves to ensure that they dress in ways that fit and reveal the gender they were assigned at birth, and demanding that they subject other Israelites to the same gender-enforcing gaze. But gender surveillance is implied by every commandment that is based on binary gender. For example, the commandment that male Gershonites must handle certain aspects of caring for the Tabernacle means that any Gershonite carrying out those duties would have to look like, act like, and be seen as male.

Every trans person knows the terror of gender surveillance, the fear that our bodies, clothing, voices, gestures—any aspect of our gender presentation—will fail to meet binary gender expectations, and the even greater fear of how others will react if they see us violating those expectations. I used to be afraid that my parents would reject me if I failed to act like the boy they thought I was; I now fear that I will be harassed, assaulted, or arrested if people on the street or in a restroom think I have failed to present myself convincingly as a woman. That surveillance happens in stores, on the street, in the workplace. It is conducted by strangers and friends, bosses and employees, police and people who are homeless, doctors and deli workers.

It's not that I think people are out to get me. Most gender surveillance is unconscious, an automatic comparison of how others look, talk, and act with our ideas of maleness and femaleness. Wherever I go, I know that others are looking at me to determine whether I am male or female, because I also engage in this constant gender surveillance. When I look in the mirror, I try to make sure (I wonder if Moses would be pleased) that others will see me as a woman, and when I look at someone else, I immediately try to determine whether they are male or female, subjecting everyone to that binary-enforcing gaze.

The spate of "bathroom bill" legislation in North Carolina and elsewhere in the second decade of the twenty-first century has drawn national attention to gender surveillance. These laws prohibit anyone from using a public restroom that doesn't correspond to the sex they were assigned at birth, adding legal penalties to the hatred directed at people who aren't recognized by others as male in a men's room or female in a women's room. The rationale for these laws is that they are necessary to protect against sexual predators: according to these laws, if I use a women's restroom despite having been born male, I am a threat to public safety.

Unlike those bathroom bills, the Levite census commandments do not criminalize priests who fail to look like the men they are supposed to be. But two chapters later, the Torah mandates another form of surveillance that, like bathroom bills, requires community members to inspect one another's bodies and expel those who do not pass inspection: "The LORD spoke to Moses, saying: 'Instruct the Israelites to remove from camp anyone with an eruption or a discharge . . . Remove male and female alike; put them outside the camp so they do not defile the camp of those in whose midst I dwell.' The Israelites did so, putting them outside the camp" (Num. 5:1–4).

Gender is not the issue here (God orders Moses to "remove male and female alike"), but like today's bathroom bills, this law demands that those whose bodies do not meet certain standards be expelled from communal spaces. They are considered threats to the community (specifically to the community's ritual purity, which their eruptions and discharge would "defile"), and so they must be removed from the camp, exiled not only from public restrooms and locker rooms but also from homes, families, workplaces, and communities.

The image of organized searches for those whose bodies are considered defiling may seem like an outgrown relic of Iron Age notions of ritual purity. But as Jews found out during the Holocaust, and as communities in the United States targeted for immigration sweeps can attest today, human beings have never left such practices behind. To my knowledge, trans people have never been subjected to this sort of communal search and removal process. But many trans people know what it's like to have others see us as defiling our families, homes, workplaces, and communities, and many of us have been driven out of them because the "eruption" of our identities is seen as a threat to communal health, harmony, religious life, or social order.

For me, the removal process began at home. When I started living as myself, I lost the right to live with my children. I could "visit" my children, as custody law puts it, but because I no longer woke them up and put them to sleep and saw them every day after school, I was removed from many aspects of their lives. When I came out as transgender after receiving tenure at Yeshiva University, I was removed from another camp, put on what the university called "involuntary research leave," which meant that I remained on the payroll but was not allowed to set foot on campus. Like ancient Israelites with an eruption or a discharge who remained Israelites even while they were removed, I was still considered part of the university, but my physical presence was treated as defiling. I was allowed to return to teaching after a year, but many transgender employees, most of whom lack the legal protection of tenure and antidiscrimination laws, are fired after they come out. When my father died a few months after I began living as myself, I experienced another form of removal: while my mother accepted my transition, she wasn't ready to have family and friends see me at my father's funeral. I stayed away, and mourned alone outside the camp.

Cruel as it may have felt to the Israelites, the removal process God commands in Numbers is in many ways less harsh than the removals many transgender people endure. Unlike today's gender-based removals, the law in Numbers doesn't suggest that those who are removed from the camp are guilty of a moral failing, sin, or crime; it targets temporary physical conditions that may affect anyone, rather than discriminating against people because of who or what they are. And though eruptions and discharges were ritually defiling, they were understood as normal consequences of being human, so being removed from the camp did not mean being rejected by family, friends, neighbors, or coworkers. After completing rituals of purification, such as those detailed in Leviticus 15:13–31, Israelites who had been removed were welcomed back, whereas today, many transgender people are expelled for years, decades—sometimes for the rest of our lives.

Traditionally religious people often claim that the Torah requires them to exclude, exile, or condemn transgender people, but the Torah never commands or encourages that kind of behavior. None of the Torah's laws requires the Israelite community to treat people whose appearance or behavior doesn't fit binary norms as defiled or defiling. Even when Moses declares that those who cross-dress are abhorrent to God, he does not say God demands that they be removed from the camp.

Because the Torah does not say that communities must punish those who violate gender norms, it creates the potential for traditional religious communities to tolerate, if not accept, trans people, even if they, like Moses, find those who do not conform to those norms abhorrent. That's what has happened at my Orthodox Jewish university. I was allowed to return to teaching after a year of being banned from campus following my transition, and, a few years later, given early promotion to full professor. Although there has been no official acceptance of me as transgender—most people, including secular colleagues, avoid even saying that word—my identity is no longer treated as a defiling condition that requires my removal. I have fewer students, but I have students, and they treat me with respect; I often feel isolated, but I never worry about being attacked or expelled. Although my transgender identity is tolerated rather than embraced, in an Orthodox institution even tolerance seems like a miracle.

As we see in the Talmudic rulings that enable intersex Jews to participate in Jewish communities, Jewish tradition recognized long ago that human beings are *not* only created male and female. The rabbis did not abandon the gender binary, or even modify it to account for people with intersex bodies. Instead, they adapted binary-based laws governing the behavior of men and women to define the do's and don'ts for intersex Jews. Similarly, my university's tolerance of me does not mean that it has abandoned or changed its commitment to the traditional gender binary. Instead, it has treated me as a woman, ignoring anything about me that doesn't fit that binary category, and remaining silent on the question of whether I am a woman, a man, or something else entirely.

The Talmud's tolerance of intersex Jews, and my university's tolerance of me as an openly transgender professor, speaks to what the Torah says—or rather, does not say—about Jews who do not fit the gender binary. There were certainly such Jews among the ancient Israelites, but the Torah ignores them. It doesn't portray them as a threat or an abomination; it doesn't declare them unclean or unfit to participate in communal worship or activities; it doesn't demonize them, curse them, punish them, push them to the margins or the shadows, order gender surveillance to guard against their entry into the community or the Tabernacle, or demand that they be expelled.

The Torah's silence opened the door for the rabbis of the Talmud to find ways for intersex Jews to be included in Jewish communities, and for my university to tolerate the presence of an openly transgender professor. In this sense, the Torah's silence speaks to the fact that people who do not fit the gender binary *can* live in—and do not defile or have to be removed from—traditional religious communities. But because the Talmud acknowledges the existence of intersex Jews, it can address questions of how binary-based customs and laws may be adapted to include community members who are not simply male or female. The Torah, however, is silent about such questions. Although it doesn't condemn transgender people, it treats us as unspeakable. Like contemporary "don't ask, don't tell" policies, the Torah allows transgender people to remain in the camp, but does not acknowledge who or what we are, or even that we are there.

Setting Oneself Apart for God:
Vows and Self-Determination in the Torah

Although the Torah doesn't speak to the fact that there are people who are not simply male or female, in the stories of Abraham, Sarah, and Jacob, it shows that people can become kinds of men and women that their families couldn't have imagined—and that God sometimes requires us to do so. But the Levite census commandments present a very different idea of gender. Unlike the stories in Genesis, they decree that Levites recorded as male devote their lives to the ritual responsibilities they are assigned along with their gender. These commandments do not allow for the possibility that individuals might be or become anything other than what they are born to be—which means they allow no room for people like Abraham, who leaves his father's house and his firstborn role, or for transgender people like me.[16]

Unlike the gender binary identities assigned by the Levite census, transgender identities are not determined by the way others see our bodies. They are determined by how transgender people see ourselves. When I say that I have identified as female since early childhood, I am not only saying that I felt like I had a body that seemed wrong; I am also saying that my sense of myself is more important in determining who I am than the identity I was assigned at birth when the nurse said, "It's a boy."

As we see in the story of Abraham, these ideas of identity are not mutually exclusive. When Abraham (then still named "Abram") abandons the role of firstborn son, he determines who he will be: not Abram, faithful son of Terah, but Abraham, faithful follower of God.[17] But in terms of his relationships with Sarah and his servants, Abraham continues to be the kind of man (a patriarch) he was born to be. Similarly, I continue to be a Jew and an American, identities that were given to me at birth, even though in living as a woman, I am determining my own life. In this regard, Abraham and I are like most human beings: our lives are determined both by the identities we were born into and by who we are to ourselves.

The Levite census commandments assume that the lives of Levite males are completely determined by roles they were assigned at birth. They do not allow Levite males to determine their lives by, say, choosing to perform the duties given to a different clan, or refusing to perform any Levite duties at all. These divinely given laws suggest that God embraces the gender binary model of identity, which holds that people are always what they are born to be. But three chapters later, in the Nazirite laws, God empowers every Israelite to determine their lives by taking vows:

> The LORD spoke to Moses, saying: "Speak to the Israelites and say to them: 'If anyone, man or woman, explicitly utters a Nazirite's vow, to set [themselves] apart for the LORD, [they] shall abstain from wine and any other intoxicant; [they] shall not drink vinegar of wine or of any other intoxicant, neither shall [they] drink anything in which grapes have been steeped, nor eat grapes fresh or dried. Throughout [their] term as Nazirite, [they] may not eat anything that is obtained from the grapevine, even seeds or skin. Throughout the term of [their] vow as Nazirite, no razor shall touch [their] head; it shall remain consecrated until the completion of [their] term as Nazirite of the LORD, the hair of [their] head being left to grow untrimmed. Throughout the term that [they] are set apart for the LORD, [they] shall not go in where there is a dead person. Even if [their] father or mother, or [their] brother or sister should die, [they] must not defile [themselves] for them, since hair set apart for [their] God is upon [their] head: throughout [their] term as Nazirite, [they are] consecrated to the LORD.'"
> (Num. 6:1–8)

These laws authorize "anyone, man or woman" to determine their own lives, as long as they do so in the specified way and for the sake of a relationship with God.[18] Although some individuals in the Torah, like Samson, are assigned to be Nazirites from birth, the vows referred to here are purely voluntary. God does not command anyone to take them, suggest that there is anything praiseworthy in becoming a Nazirite, or offer any religious or spiritual benefit for doing so. And though God determines what Nazirites must do, it is up to individuals to determine, for reasons of their own, whether or not to become one.

Like many transgender people today, those who took Nazirite vows changed their behavior and appearance in ways that violated social norms, marking themselves as different and setting themselves apart from those around them. Nazirites were not allowed to taste any part or product of grapevines, even though grapes were one of the Israelites' staple agricultural products. They weren't allowed to cut their hair, and even if a close relative died, they couldn't go near the body.

According to Jewish law, someone could become a Nazirite at any time, without any preparation or explanation.[19] Some Israelites, no doubt, were unhappy when a parent or child or business partner or friend suddenly stopped cutting their hair, refused to drink wine together or participate in the grape harvest, and stayed away when others were tending to or mourning over the body of someone who had died. But the Nazirite laws not only tell Nazirites what to do; they also make it clear that God expects other Israelites to accept the self-determination of those who take Nazirite vows and the strange, even antisocial actions through which Nazirite identity was expressed. No matter how angry, inconvenienced, or baffled Israelites might have been when those close to them chose to take Nazirite vows, no matter how greatly those vows disrupted Nazirites' families or interfered with the roles they were expected to play as fathers or mothers, daughters or sons, the Nazirite laws require others to respect Nazirites' behavior.

If my son and I had been ancient Israelites and I had upended our lives not through gender transition but by taking Nazirite vows, the Nazirite laws would have helped me explain, and helped him understand, the changes that set me apart from him, from our family, and from the life we had shared. If he asked why I was growing out my hair, I would have said, "Because this is what the Torah says Nazirites must do." If he asked why I had decided to become a Nazirite, I would have said, "Because, as other Israelites sometimes do, I realized that I had to change my life to express my relationship with God." If he worried whether, now that I was living as a Nazirite, I was a different person, I would have reassured him that the Torah makes it clear that becoming a Nazirite does not erase who we are—that though I looked and acted differently, I was still his father.

My son might still have been angry and embarrassed that I had become a Nazirite. But he would understand that the ways in which I had changed myself and my life were valid, authentic, even sacred. He would have grown up knowing that Nazirite self-determination is permitted by God and the

Torah. And he would know that despite the ways they set themselves apart, Nazirites remain the parents, children, friends, coworkers, neighbors, and members of the community they were before they took their vows, that becoming a Nazirite does not mean rejecting, abandoning, or betraying those they love.

But though the Nazirite laws require Israelites to accept Nazirites' vows, they don't suggest how to resolve the conflicts that must have arisen when their acts of self-determination disrupted their families. Like many transgender people, I know those sorts of conflicts well. My family was ripped apart by them. I don't know whether ancient Israelites ever married with the understanding that they would someday take Nazirite vows, but I certainly didn't get married with the understanding that I would someday embark on gender transition. Although I came out to my now ex-wife as a transsexual long before we married, we both believed that I would keep living as a man no matter how much pain my gender dysphoria caused me, because we both knew that if I decided to live as myself, my marriage would end, friends would turn away, and I would probably lose my job.

The fear of those consequences, all of which came to pass to one degree or another, made us cling to the life we had built around my male identity long after it was clear that I was physically and emotionally breaking down under the strain of living as someone I wasn't. If I had been diagnosed with a life-threatening illness, my wife and everyone we knew would have insisted that I get medical treatment, even if that treatment disrupted our family. But no matter how much it hurt me to live as a man, everyone expected me to do so until the day I died. I agreed: I believed that I owed it to my family to live as the man they loved even if it killed me, or, as was becoming more likely by the day, it drove me to kill myself.

Those who support transgender people's struggles—friends, therapists, support groups, political organizations, blogs, and books—tend to speak as though our right to determine our own identities is all that matters, regardless of how our families may be affected by our gender transition. Those who oppose the expression of trans identities tend to say the reverse: what matters most is family, community, and tradition, and transgender people must be willing to sacrifice ourselves to maintain them. To the first group, my transition made me a hero; to the second, it showed that I was a man so self-obsessed that I didn't care how much I hurt my wife and children as long as I pleased myself. None of these voices acknowledged that I, as a transgender person who was also a husband and father, could neither ignore my family's needs nor continue to erase myself for their sakes. None of them could help me think through the devastating choice between being true to myself and being true to those I loved.

In the laws regarding women's vows, however, the Torah speaks directly to the conflict between self-determination and traditional gender roles. As we see in the Nazirite laws, the Torah gives women the power to change their lives by taking religious vows, but as we see in many other laws, it also assumes that most women live under the authority of fathers or husbands. In Numbers 30:4–15, the Torah addresses the conflicts that arise when women exercise their power of self-determination by taking vows that change their lives in ways their husbands or fathers do not like. The Torah could have prevented such conflicts from arising by prohibiting vows by women living under male authority, or it could have taken the opposite approach, ruling that women's vows stand no matter how husbands or fathers feel about them. Like today's one-sided arguments over transgender identities, such one-sided decisions would have treated self-determination and family obligations as mutually exclusive, preserving one at the expense of the other.

Instead, the Torah attempts to resolve the family conflicts that may arise from women's vows in a way that supports both women's power of self-determination and patriarchal family order. Women who live under male authority are permitted to make vows, such as vows to live as Nazirites, but those vows only become binding if their fathers or husbands do not object to them the same day they find out about them (Num. 30:5, 8, 12). If they object promptly, the vows are annulled: the women who made them are not obligated to fulfill them, and they will be forgiven by God for failing to do so (Num. 30:6, 9, 13). If patriarchs don't voice their objections promptly, women's vows stand, regardless of how husbands or fathers feel about them.

But even when they annul them, patriarchs don't have the power to void women's vows, or the relationships with God those vows express.[20] By assuring a woman whose vows are annulled that "the LORD will forgive her" (Num. 30:6), God shows that women's vetoed vows are still taken seriously, as commitments that need to be forgiven.

Unlike the arguments I heard for and against my right to live as myself, the Torah addresses the family conflicts raised by women's self-determination without taking sides. It doesn't say that women should forgo their vows for the sake of their families, or that men should not object to them. It doesn't label women who make vows that disrupt their families as selfish, or men who annul them as tyrants. Rather than blaming or moralizing, the Torah presents the conflict between self-determination and gender roles as a normal part of family life, and refuses to choose one over the other: it recognizes, protects, and limits both patriarchal authority and women's power of self-determination.

I don't share the Torah's concern with preserving patriarchal authority, but in the laws of women's vows, the Torah models the kind of perspective I longed for during my gender transition, one that would honor both my need for self-determination and my wife's need for me to remain the man she counted on me to be. That perspective would not have resolved the conflict that tore my family apart, but it could have helped us understand it, discuss it, and seek our own version of the kind of compromise the Torah offers: a compromise that is pragmatic rather than moralistic, that seeks a mutually respectful give-and-take rather than surrender on one side or the other. I don't know whether we would have found such a compromise—after all, as the Torah recognizes elsewhere, some marital conflicts can only be resolved by divorce—but by prompting us to search for one, the Torah could have helped us avoid years of bitterness, blame, and recrimination.

The laws governing women's vows are as dry and practical as any family court decree, but they speak to a profoundly spiritual question, one that I am often asked: how can I reconcile my relationship with God and my transgender identity? These laws acknowledge that even acts of self-determination that disrupt our families can be sacred. They make it clear that the God who speaks the language of patriarchy and binary gender throughout the Torah also empowers individuals to leave the roles and identities we are born to and set ourselves apart for the God who dwells in the wilderness beyond them. And they require even the most traditional religious communities to accept that when it comes to relationships with God, all of us, even those most bound by gender—women under patriarchal authority—have the power of self-determination, the God-given power to be what we will be.

Festival of Binaries

Even though the laws of Nazirite and women's vows support the idea that human lives are not soley determined by the gender roles we are born to, the Torah never questions the assumption that human beings are only and always male or female. Indeed, from the beginning of Genesis, when the man and the woman eat the fruit of the Tree of the Knowledge of Good and Evil, to the end of Deuteronomy, when Moses begs the Israelites to choose life over death and blessing over curse, the Torah describes human lives in binary terms.

When I was a child, I did my best to ignore that aspect of the Torah, but every spring, when Passover came, I was forced to change my life to fit the Torah's binaries. My middle-class, minimally religious American family didn't have much in common with the Israelite slaves who, according to the Torah, celebrated the first Passover on the eve of leaving Egypt. But because my family identified as Jewish, we still felt bound by the laws of Passover given to those slaves in chapter 12 of Exodus:

> This day [the day of the Exodus from Egypt] shall be to you one of remembrance: you shall celebrate it as a festival to the LORD throughout the ages; you shall celebrate it as an institution for all time. Seven days you shall eat unleavened bread; on the very first day you shall remove leaven from your houses, for whoever eats leavened bread from the first day to the seventh day, that person shall be cut off from Israel. . . .
>
> In the first month, from the fourteenth day of the month at evening, you shall eat unleavened bread until the twenty-first day of the month at evening. No leaven shall be found in your houses for seven days. For whoever eats what is leavened, that person shall be cut off from the community of Israel, whether he is a stranger or

a citizen of the country. You shall eat nothing leavened; in all your settlements you shall eat unleavened bread. (Exod. 12:14–5, 18–20)

For my family, as for the ancient Israelites, observing Passover meant upending our lives to fit the binary distinctions these laws impose: distinctions between leavened food, which is forbidden during the festival, and unleavened food, which is permitted; between the insides of houses, which must be leaven-free during the festival, and the outside world, which is not governed by the laws of Passover; between Passover, when distinctions between leavened and unleavened become crucial, and the rest of the year, when they don't matter at all; and, most importantly, between Jews (or, as the Torah says, "Israelites"), who are obligated to observe the laws of Passover, and non-Jews, who are not.

These laws are the Torah's equivalent of "Jewish Identity for Dummies." Many Jews find it hard to follow the complex system of Jewish law that grew out of centuries of rabbinic discussion. But all Jews, even children, can grasp binary distinctions like this. Food is either leavened or unleavened; leaven is either inside our houses or it isn't; people are either Jews, who have to celebrate Passover, or they are not. Passover is literally a festival of binaries, a festival we celebrate by changing our lives to fit Passover's either/or terms.[21]

The laws of the first Passover not only established a new festival; they also established a new definition of Israelite identity. According to those laws, only those who celebrated the festival and marked their doorposts with blood on the evening before the Exodus would be identified by God as Israelites; only their houses would be passed over, spared, during the plague of the firstborn (Exod. 12:11–13).

But before the first Passover, Israelites were identified not by religion but by ancestry:[22] to be an Israelite (or "Hebrew"—the Torah seems to use both terms interchangeably) was to be a descendant of Abraham, Isaac, and Jacob.[23] And as we see in the story of Moses, identifying as an Israelite did not mean that one could not identify in other ways as well. Moses was born to Israelite parents but adopted and raised by an Egyptian princess, and in the one glimpse the Torah gives of his life in Egypt, it is clear that Moses identifies as both Israelite and Egyptian: "[W]hen Moses had grown up, he went out to his kinfolk and witnessed their labors. He saw an Egyptian beating a Hebrew, one of his kinsmen. He turned this way and that and, seeing no one about, he struck down the Egyptian and hid him in the sand. When he went out the next day, he found two Hebrews fighting; so he said to the offender, 'Why do you strike your fellow?' He retorted, 'Who made you chief and ruler over us? Do you mean to kill me as you killed the Egyptian?'" (Exod. 2:11–14).

As verse 11 tells us, Moses considers the enslaved Israelites his kinfolk. That identification leads him to intervene violently when he sees one of them being beaten. But in striking down the Egyptian, Moses acts like a high-handed Egyptian prince, and when he attempts to break up a fight among Israelites the next day, it is clear that they see him not as one of them but as an Egyptian. Moses, realizing that others know about the murder he committed, flees to Midian, but even in exile, he continues to be identified as an Egyptian: after he helps the daughters of a local priest, they tell their father that "an Egyptian rescued us" (Exod. 2:19).

Moses's identity becomes even more complicated when he marries one of those daughters, Tzipporah, and lives for decades as a member of her family. We don't know how Moses thought of himself during those years, but it is clear in the dialogue at the burning bush that he does not strongly identify as an Israelite (Exod. 3:7–15).[24] God refers to the Israelites as "My people" rather than as "your [Moses's] people," and neither of them says anything that suggests that Moses is concerned about the suffering of the Israelites or how to end it. The sense of kinship that led Moses to intervene when he saw a fellow Israelite being beaten and when he saw Israelites arguing is so far behind him that even though his family is still enslaved, his only interest in God's plans for liberation is making sure he doesn't have to be part of them. Moses begs God to "make someone else Your agent" (Exod. 4:13), and he makes it clear that he believes that if he did return to Egypt, the Israelites would reject him as an outsider, rather than embracing him as one of their own (Exod. 4:1–13).

As we see in these portrayals of Moses, before the first Passover commandments were given, being an Israelite and being a non-Israelite were not mutually exclusive. The young Moses identifies as both Hebrew and Egyptian; the Moses we see at the burning bush doesn't identify strongly as either. The laws of the first Passover strengthen Israelite identity by making it a matter of religion as well as ancestry, and by making the distinction between Israelites and non-Israelites a matter of life and death: "For that night [the night of the first Passover] I will go through the land of Egypt and strike down every firstborn in the land of Egypt. And the blood on the houses where you are staying shall be a sign for you: when I see the blood I will pass over you, so that no plague will destroy you when I strike the land of Egypt" (Exod. 12:12–13).

In this passage, God divides Egyptian society into two mutually exclusive, binary categories: Israelites, who observe the commandment to mark their houses with the blood of the Passover sacrifice, and non-Israelites, who don't. God leaves no room for the kinds of in-between, fluid, intersectional, or queer forms of Israelite identity we see in Moses's story, or recognize any distinctions among non-Israelites in terms of ethnicity, economic class, or political power. Everyone had to identify as Israelite or non-Israelite, a choice that, on the night of the first Passover, was literally a choice between life and death, blessing and curse (Deut. 30:19). From the highest levels of Egyptian society to the lowest, "from the firstborn of Pharaoh who sat on the throne to the firstborn of the captive who was in the dungeon," those who did not identify themselves as Israelites by ritually marking their houses with blood were treated by God as non-Israelites even if they were Israelite by ancestry: among them, the Torah tells us, "there was no house where there was not someone dead" (Exod. 12:29, 30).

Although my family didn't mark our doorposts with blood when we celebrated Passover—that requirement seems to have applied only to the first Passover—like the ancient Israelites, we observed the festival to express our identification as Jews; like the Israelites who marked their houses with blood, we defined being Jewish in simple, binary terms. To us, humanity consisted of Jews and non-Jews; everyone was either one or the other.

My family didn't keep kosher, but we still went to the trouble of eradicating leaven from our house and diets during Passover. As a boy, I wasn't expected to help with my mother's backbreaking pre-Passover cleaning, but Passover's binaries still descended on me like a plague. I hated matzah and everything made with it, particularly the peanut butter and jelly sandwiches

I took to school, which exploded in a sticky shower of crumbs when I tried to eat them.

But there was one thing I liked about Passover. Most of the year, I seemed to be the only one worrying about binaries and identity. The laws of Passover require every Jew to think about binaries and worry about whether we are or are not managing to fit our messy lives within them, because, during the festival, those binaries define whether or not we are the Jews we are supposed to be. The plague of the firstborn only happened once, but the laws of the first Passover enforce a high-stakes definition of Israelite identity every year, decreeing that anyone who eats leaven during the festival "shall be cut off from the community of Israel" (Exod. 12:19). My life was defined by my fear that I would do something that might reveal that I wasn't the boy I was pretending to be, and be cut off from my family; the laws of Passover call for every Jew to worry about doing something—eating leaven during the festival—that will cut them off not only from their families but also from the Jewish people.

The Torah ratchets up the anxiety promoted by Passover's binaries by decreeing that the festival begins "at twilight" (Exod. 12:6). Twilight, of course, is a time that does not fit within binary categories: it is a time between day and night, a time that is both, and neither. That is a terribly vague starting signal for laws that, if violated, can lead to being cut off from the community of Israel.

The rabbis, acutely aware of the danger of beginning Passover's identity-defining taboo against leaven at such an inexact time, added several preliminary stages to the onset of the festival, creating close to twenty-four hours that in some ways are Passover (in the sense that leaven is no longer supposed to be in our dwellings) and in some ways are not (because the holiday hasn't actually begun). For example, they ruled that the final ritual search to eliminate traces of leaven from the home, the *bedikat hametz*, should take place the night before the festival—before the prohibition against possessing leaven begins. This search is designed to render homes almost, but not quite, leaven-free; a pile of crumbs is preserved in the home overnight and burned the next morning. The rabbis also decided that during that morning, Jews could eat either leavened or unleavened bread, but during the afternoon before the festival begins, they are not permitted to eat either. These additional laws help ensure that no one will inadvertently possess or eat leaven once the festival begins at twilight, but in order to do so, they blur the Torah's binary distinction between time that is and time that is not Passover.

As the rabbis recognized, other binary distinctions established by the laws of Passover—distinctions that seem clear and simple in the Torah—are also hard to maintain in practice. For example, the fundamental distinction between what is leavened and what is not leavened is complicated by the fact that yeast, which causes leavening, is an airborne organism that cannot actually be removed from or kept out of houses, no matter how intensively we clean them. Whenever yeast lands on unbaked flour, leavening may, invisibly, begin—so the rabbis reinforced the Torah's prohibition against possessing leaven during the festival by forbidding the possession of grain that could accidentally leaven. Ashkenazic rabbis went even further, prohibiting many starches that can't be leavened, such as rice, beans, and corn, so that Jews would not mistake grains that leaven for starches that do not. These prohibitions create a binary-confounding category of foods, called *kitniyot*, that are to be treated like leaven even though they cannot be leavened. Different Jewish communities adopted different definitions of *kitniyot*, so that what the Torah presents as a simple binary distinction—"No leaven shall be found in your houses for seven days. For whoever eats what is leavened, that person shall be cut off from the community of Israel"—has become a tangle of regulations that vary from community to community and family to family.

The rabbis also saw the difficulty of maintaining the binary distinction between what is in our houses and what is outside them. As anyone who has ever cleaned house in preparation for Passover knows, bits of what is outside our houses—which may include bits of what is leavened—are constantly being brought inside them, tracked in on the bottoms of shoes, blown in through the window, and so on. The rabbis addressed that problem by adding a legal declaration, to be recited at the conclusion of the ritual search for leaven on the night before Passover and repeated as part of the ritual of burning the remaining crumbs the next morning, that any leaven remaining in the house is "ownerless as the dust of the earth." This declaration relieves the fears of anxious house cleaners by blurring the binary distinction between having and not having leaven in one's home during the festival, creating a third category of leaven that is not considered to be in our possession even though it is in our homes.[25]

These rabbinic rulings recognize how hard it is to make messy human lives fit binary distinctions—so hard that the rabbis, in an effort to help Jews keep the laws of Passover, complicate the simple either/ors those laws define by adding non-binary categories such as leaven we have but do not possess, and hours when Passover has and hasn't begun. As the rabbis who complicated them recognized, even as the laws of Passover strengthen Jewish identity by dividing the world into Jews and non-Jews, they also render Jewish identity extremely fragile, putting every Jew one bite of leaven away from being cut off from the community of Israel.[26]

Most of my life was blighted by the fear that I would be cut off for doing or saying something that would show that I didn't fit the binary that defined me as a male. The laws of the first Passover are designed to give every Jew a taste of that kind of fear, the fear that we will violate the binary terms for identity and be cut off from the community of Israel. The more strictly identity-defining binaries are enforced, the more anxiety they generate, because we know how easy it is to violate them and cut ourselves off from the communities that enforce them. The more strictly we try to follow the laws of Passover, the more anxious we are likely to feel, and the more directly we will confront the impossibility of making human reality—crumb-accumulating houses, airborne yeast, foods that look like foods that are forbidden—conform to the binaries these laws impose, which is why the rabbis complicated those binaries beyond recognition.

But it wasn't only the rabbis who noticed the mismatch between Passover's binary categories and the complexity of human lives. Even in the laws of the first Passover, God recognizes that the distinction between Israelites and non-Israelites created by those laws is much more complicated than that binary suggests. For example, in Exodus 12:19, God extends the taboo against eating leaven during Passover to *gerim*, "strangers," resident aliens who live among Israelites but are not Israelites by ancestry. Even though *gerim* are not considered Israelites, God considers them so connected to the community of Israel that if they violate the prohibition against eating leaven they must be cut off from it.[27] The distinction between Israelites and non-Israelites gets even messier in the laws regarding who may eat the Passover sacrifice: "This is the law of the Passover offering: No foreigner shall eat of it. But any slave a man has bought may eat of it once he has been circumcised. . . . If a stranger who dwells with you would offer the Passover to the LORD, all his males must be circumcised; then he shall be admitted to offer it; he shall then be as a citizen of the country" (Exod. 12:43–44, 48).

At first, the law of the Passover offering is a model of binary simplicity: no foreigner (i.e., non-Israelite) is permitted to eat the Passover sacrifice. But God immediately blurs the Israelite/non-Israelite binary by allowing two categories of non-Israelites to eat the sacrifice: circumcised non-Israelite slaves owned by Israelites, and "strangers" who have circumcised all the males in their households. Even here, in the laws of a festival that celebrates the binary distinction between Israelites and non-Israelites, God considers it more important to include non-Israelites who identify with the community of Israel than to preserve the purity and simplicity of binary categories by excluding anyone who does not fit within them.[28]

These laws show that God knows what transgender people know: the binaries that make identities seem clear and simple, easy to express and enforce, are, in practice, impossible to maintain, because they do not and cannot fit the complexity of human lives and human communities. Of course, as we saw in chapter 1, it is precisely because reality is so complex that human beings embrace the simplicity of binaries. In a world in which, as the plagues and miracles of the Exodus remind us, everything we think we know can change in an instant, the binary distinctions imposed by the laws of Passover can be a comfort, even if they aren't comfortable. And though the plague of the firstborn is now millennia behind us, we still live in a world in which the distinction between who is Jewish and who is not, between who is "us" and who is "them," can be a matter of life and death.[29]

The Torah doesn't acknowledge the difficulties caused by the pressure to fit messy human lives into the either/or categories of the gender binary. But in both the laws of Passover and contemporary debates over transgender identities, we see the same dilemma: how to respond to the fact that there are always people who do not fit the binary categories on which we base identities, relationships, and communities. Contemporary debates over trans identity tend to circle around the same three possible responses: forcing everyone to conform to binary gender categories (and expelling—cutting off from the community—those who refuse); expanding our conception of gender by adding new gender categories; or eliminating binary gender altogether. In the laws regarding who may eat the Passover sacrifice, God takes the middle path: instead of enforcing or eliminating the Israelite/non-Israelite binary, God adds additional categories to accommodate those who identify with Israel strongly enough to want to participate in religious rituals but who were not born or raised as Israelites.

God's example sets a scriptural precedent for religious communities wrestling with whether, and how, to include people who do not fit binary categories. But even if we don't see God's modification of the Israelite/non-Israelite binary in the Passover sacrifice laws as an example for how to accommodate transgender people, it is clear here that God does not consider binary categories, even those established by God, as so sacred that religious communities must exclude anyone who does not fit them.

In Passover's identity-defining binaries and God's exceptions to them, the Torah speaks both to my oldest fear and to my deepest wish as a transgender person. My fear has always been that binary categories are so essential to human identity that communities cannot afford to include people like me who do not fit within them. My wish is that, as God does in the Passover sacrifice laws, the communities I consider mine will be willing to sacrifice the simplicity of binary identities to enable people like me to add our joy to their celebrations, our voices to their songs, our strength to their struggles, our lives to their lives.

As God shows in the laws of the Passover sacrifice, it is possible to expand identity-defining binaries, even those that we consider sacred and essential to our communities, to accommodate people who do not fit within them. But no matter how we alter human categories, there is one stranger we can never accommodate: God. Even when dwelling in the midst of the Israelite community God created to be a nation of priests, God remains an incomprehensible stranger, who, as Maimonides insists, does not fit human categories, including those that God has decreed. God defines Israelite identity through innumerable binaries, but cannot fit any of them. God is neither circumcised nor uncircumcised, neither Israelite nor non-Israelite, neither eats nor abstains from eating leaven during Passover, and cannot fulfill Moses's injunction to choose life or death, blessing or curse, because God is the source of all these things, and subject to none of them. God creates the world and all that is in it, but as a famous rabbinic saying declares, "God is the place of the world, but the world is not God's place."[30]

The Torah speaks to transgender lives because so much of it speaks to how hard it is for humanity to recognize and embrace someone—God—who cannot fit human terms. Transgender perspectives illuminate the Torah because we, like God, know what it means to love those who cannot understand us, to dwell in the midst of communities that have no place for us, to present ourselves in human terms that cannot help but misrepresent us.[31] Religious communities that welcome transgender people hear in our voices an echo of the loneliness that haunts the living word of God. Religious communities that treat openly transgender people, even those of us who have lived in those communities all our lives, as strangers, should recall that God repeatedly commands the Israelites to remember their own experiences of being treated as strangers in the land of Egypt: to remember that they know—because God wants communities devoted to God to know—the soul of the stranger.

FIVE

KNOWING THE SOUL OF THE STRANGER

"How Long Will This People Spurn Me?"

When I first turned to it as a child, the Torah seemed like a series of stories about how hard it is for God to have relationships with human beings. Like me, I believed, God was too different, too strange, for human beings to relate to, and that belief, despairing as it was, made me feel less alone.

Before my gender transition, I had never experienced a relationship in which my differences were accepted, because I hid the ways in which I was different. But as I grew up, it became hard to ignore the fact that the Torah portrays relationships in which individual human beings (notably Abraham and Moses) accept God's differences and are able to relate to God even though, like me, God does not fit human categories. However, when it came to being recognized and accepted not by individuals but by human communities, it still seemed to me that the Torah portrays God as being little more successful than I was. From Exodus to the end of II Chronicles, the Torah is filled with examples of the Israelites' failures to recognize and remember that God is there, dwelling among them.

The most striking of those failures occur after the Exodus, when God's place in the Israelite community should be absolutely clear. God creates the Israelite community by bringing them out of Egypt; maintains it by giving them manna every day; and rules it not only through the laws God communicates via Moses, but also through the pillars of smoke and fire whose movements guide the community on its journey. When God gives the Ten Commandments, God speaks directly to each and every Israelite. The entire people, camped around Mount Sinai, hears God deliver laws governing the most intimate aspects of their daily lives: when they should work and when they should rest, how they should treat their parents and one another. Even after God stops talking, the Torah tells us that it should still be clear to the Israelites that God is there, because "the Presence of the LORD appeared in the sight of the Israelites as a consuming fire on the top of the mountain" (Exod. 25:17).

But after Moses disappears into the cloud that covers Mount Sinai, the Israelites no longer recognize the God whose presence is blazing on the peak above them. Instead,

> When the people saw that Moses was so long in coming down from the mountain, the people gathered against Aaron and said to him, "Come, make us a god who shall go before us, for that man Moses, who brought us from the land of Egypt—we do not know what has happened to him.
>
> [Aaron] made . . . a molten calf. And they exclaimed, "This is your god, O Israel, who brought you out of the land of Egypt!" (Exod. 32:1, 4)

The Israelites don't just fail to recognize that God is there; they also seem to have forgotten God's role in their history and their lives, first claiming that Moses brought them out of Egypt, and then creating an idol—the infamous Golden Calf—to worship as the divinity who delivered them from Egypt. Despite all that God has done for them, it seems to the Israelites as though God was never there.

The Torah emphasizes that the Israelites' amnesia about God doesn't extend to Moses. They remember the role Moses played in the Exodus, they notice his absence, wait for his return, and panic when he is gone so long. Moses has a unique place in the Israelite community, but unlike God, he *has* a place, an identity, a family, a tribe, and roles—husband, father, younger brother, organizer, leader—that define who he is and where he stands in the community and ensure that he is noticed when present and missed when absent.

But even though God's presence is blazing before them, God, unlike Moses, has no place in Israelite society, no fixed role or identity, not even a form, like Moses's body or the Golden Calf, by which to be recognized or remembered. When the Israelites left Egypt, they didn't see God's presence appear as fire—in fact, the Torah doesn't tell us that God appeared in a visible form to them at all—and so even though God's presence is blazing in front of them, they don't realize that the God who brought them out of Egypt is there. In fact, once Moses is out of sight, the Israelites don't seem to remember God's role in the Exodus. In the Torah's telling, it is clear that it is God, not Moses, who brings the Israelites out of Egypt. That makes the Israelites' inability to recognize and even remember God's presence seem willful, as though they are turning their backs on God, denying that God is and was with them.[1]

But when I think of my family when I was growing up, I see another explanation. I have no place in my family's history of my childhood. The real me—me as I knew myself when I was a child—doesn't appear in my family's snapshots or stories. I was there, with my fear and misery and longing to be loved, but no one could recognize and so no one can remember the girl who had no body, the invisible daughter and sister who, as far as my family was concerned, didn't exist because she had never been born. The child I showed my family, the one who appears in their memories, stories, and photographs, was the boy I pretended to be, an image I knew they could recognize, relate to, and love because it fit their ideas of gender, just as the Israelites could recognize, relate to, and worship the Golden Calf because, unlike the God whose presence is blazing on the mountain, it fit their ideas of divinity.

I gave my family an image of a child they could understand, and because I loved them, I tried to pretend, to myself and to them, that when they loved that image they were loving me. They, in turn, gave that image a clear, secure place in our family. They fed and clothed it, sent it to school, took it on vacations, and framed photos of it (several still hang on my mother's wall).

But as God makes clear at the beginning of the Ten Commandments, God will not settle for that kind of relationship with the Israelites. God demands that the Israelites recognize and give a place not to an image that fits their ideas of divinity, but to God's formless, incomprehensible, category-disrupting presence: "I the LORD am your God who brought you out of the land of Egypt, the house of bondage: You shall have no other gods besides Me. You shall not make for yourself a sculptured image, or any likeness of what is in the heavens above, or on the earth below, or in the waters under the earth. You shall not bow down to them or serve them" (Exod. 20:2–5).

These words are so familiar that it is easy to forget that even as God prohibits the Israelites from making or worshipping images of divinity, God is also demonstrating how utterly strange God is, different not just from other, more familiar deities, but also from everything the Israelites know. God's voice emerges not from a body but from thunder and flame; God's presence shakes the mountain. As God's self-introduction reminds the Israelites, this is the God who turned water into blood, day into night, dust into swarming lice; who split a sea in half and led them across on dry land. Not only is God unlike anything in the heavens, the earth, or the waters: God does not fit and has no place in any human or natural order.

No wonder the Israelites find it hard to recognize or remember God when Moses is not there to remind them. God insists on being known and worshipped only as a being they cannot imagine. In Moses's absence, the Israelites lose their sense of God's presence, and fulfill their desire for a god to lead them by making the Golden Calf. The Golden Calf gives the Israelites a version of divinity that makes sense: it looks the way they expect it to look and it means what they say it means; it goes where they take it, stays where they put it, and fits the roles they assign it. The Golden Calf will never disrupt the laws of nature or the order of the community; it will never lead the Israelites beyond what they know and understand; it will never shake the foundations of their world by saying to them, "I am."

The image of a boy I fashioned fit my family's ideas so well that they never missed me. The Golden Calf fits the Israelites' ideas of divinity so well that even though it is made out of their own jewelry, before their eyes, they immediately embrace it as the god who brought them out of Egypt. The Golden Calf fills the empty place in their history and their lives where they know divinity should be, and if God and Moses had not intervened, there is no sign that the Israelites would have ever missed God's presence. To me, this is the most horrifying aspect of the Israelites' idolatry: not their disobedience, but the fact that, like my family, they prefer a relationship with an image they understand to a relationship with a real being they can't.

But though enraged by the Golden Calf, God does not give up on having a place in Israelite society, and despite their flirtation with idolatry, the Israelites make it clear that they want God's presence to remain among them. They not only repent, they go into mourning when God, after punishing them with a plague, says, "I will not go in your midst . . . lest I destroy you" (Exod. 33:3, 4). They now prefer to live with an incomprehensible God who might destroy them than to accept a safer, smaller version of divinity, such as the angel God offers to lead them (Exod. 33:2).

When God summons Moses back into the cloud covering Mount Sinai, the Israelites wait faithfully below (Exod. 34:28–33). When Moses returns, they are so eager for God to dwell among them that, as the last five chapters of Exodus detail, they enthusiastically contribute the materials and labor necessary to fulfill God's design for the Tabernacle, the portable sanctuary that gives God's presence a clear, well-defined place in their camp: "For over the Tabernacle a cloud of the LORD rested by day, and fire would appear in it by night, in the view of all the house of Israel throughout their journeys" (Exod. 40:38).

The Tabernacle represents the most complete integration of God into a human community recorded in the Torah.[2] Although God continues to appear in other, unpredictable ways, once the Tabernacle is completed, the Israelites can always count on finding the cloud and fire that signify God's presence there. When they think back on their journeys through the wilderness, the consistency of those signs—signs that, though miraculous, take forms they can recognize and understand—enable them to remember that God, the same God, has always been with them.

But despite God's and the Israelites' joint efforts to give God a place in the Israelite community, even after the Tabernacle is completed, the Israelites continue to complain, cower, and despair as though they don't know or remember the God who dwells in their midst. To take the most infamous of many examples, the Israelites refuse God's command to occupy Canaan. "Why is the LORD taking us to that land to fall by the sword? Our wives and children will be carried off," they wail, after hearing the spies' descriptions of the strength of Canaan's inhabitants (Num. 14:2–3). "If only we had died in the land of Egypt . . . or if only we might die in the wilderness," they shout. "It would be better for us to go back to Egypt!" (Num. 14:2–3). They would rather be dead or enslaved than count on God to help them.

God takes the Israelites' refusal as a personal rejection, asking Moses, "How long will this people spurn Me, and how long will they have no faith in Me despite all the signs that I have performed in their midst?" (Num. 14:11). As God says, the Israelites are acting as though they don't know and can't trust the God who visibly dwells at the center of their community and is intimately involved in their lives.

Unlike their behavior in making the Golden Calf, the Israelites do not refuse to enter Canaan because they have forgotten God's presence. They acknowledge in their wailing that they know the God telling them to occupy Canaan is the God who brought them out of Egypt. But they also know that they don't understand God and can't predict what God will do. The Israelites may not know that Moses had to convince God not to wipe them out for the sin of the Golden Calf, but they have repeatedly seen the God who sustains them with manna also kill many of them in outbursts of anger. God's initial response to the Israelites' refusal to begin the occupation of Canaan shows that the Israelites are right to worry that they cannot count on God to fulfill the role of resident benevolent deity. After asking Moses, "How long will this people have no faith in Me despite all the signs I have performed in their midst?" the God who is supposed to protect the Israelites in Canaan once again turns violently against them: "I will strike them with pestilence and disown them, and I will make of you [Moses] a nation far more numerous than they!" (Num. 14:12).

God can, and does, threaten and punish the Israelites into obedience, but God's threats and punishments cannot change the fact that even while dwelling in their midst, God remains a stranger to them, a being whose motives, feelings, and perspective they cannot understand, who cannot be counted on to share their values (even values as simple as the desire to protect their families from heavily armed Canaanites), a being so different that, despite the Tabernacle and their shared history, they do not see God as part of their community. The Israelites treat God as a stranger not because they don't know God, but because they do.

The Torah makes it hard to side with the Israelites in these confrontations, but their treatment of God fit my lifelong assumption that God and I were simply too different to fit into human communities. If God had asked me, "How long will this people spurn Me?," I would have answered, sometimes in rage, often in anguish, always in despair, "Forever." The Is-raelites spurn God, I thought, because people are people, and neither God nor I could ever find a place among them.

Although they too are often driven to despair by the Israelites' behavior, Moses and the biblical prophets who followed him disagree with me. In Deuteronomy, Moses claims that it is not hard for the Israelites to give God a place at the center of Israelite community: "And now, O Israel, what does the LORD your God demand of you? Only this: to revere the LORD your God, to walk only in [God's] paths, to love [God], and to serve the LORD your God with all your heart and soul, keeping the LORD's commandments and laws" (Deut. 10:12–13). According to this view, which is echoed in dif-ferent variations by later prophets, God's place in Israelite community is clear, and relating to God is simple: God is to be revered, loved, and served by following the laws and commandments. No understanding of God, no negotiation of God's differences, is required for the Israelites to relate to God. As long as the Israelites do as they have been told to do, they will be living in ways that show that they acknowledge and accept the God in their midst. According to this view, because it is so simple for the Israelites to give God a place at the center of their community, when they don't, it is not because God is too different to fit in, or because God makes demands (such as invading the heavily armed land of Canaan) that make no sense from the Israelites' perspective, but because they are too sinful, stubborn, ungrateful, stupid, greedy, or otherwise damnably determined not to do so.[3]

Many of the prophets express a dim view of human beings in general and Israelites in particular, but even their most passionate condemnations of the Israelites' treatment of God reflect an optimism that I couldn't un-derstand. To me, it was obvious that God could never have a place in hu-man community; the prophets insist that God can, that as soon as human beings turn away from our sins, we will find it easy to remember and act as though God is there, dwelling among us.

I loved the prophets' idealism, but what they said didn't seem to have much to do with the people I knew. I didn't see the human beings around me as choosing to reject or turn away from God. Although they didn't seem to know that God was there, it wasn't because they were evil or con-sumed by sin, and they certainly didn't deserve the plagues, exiles, and other punishments the prophets prescribe as cures for neglecting God's presence. They didn't know that God was there because God was invisible and incomprehensible, with no body to make room for, no role in their lives, not even a shadow they might notice stretching beside their own.

God's estrangement from human communities is not a moral or modern or secular problem; it isn't caused by mass media, the internet, the rise of science, the decline of the traditional family, or defects in faith or worship or theology. It is built into God's relationships with human beings. Being a member of a human community means taking on roles and identities, acting consistently, and being seen and known in ways that are understandable and predictable. God can't do that. As God says at the beginning of the Ten Commandments, God can only be known as someone—something—human beings do not and cannot know. If communities treat God as a deity we understand, a deity who fulfills the roles we assign and appears in forms we recognize, we are repeating our own version of the making of the Golden Calf. If we don't recognize God's incomprehensible strangeness, we aren't recognizing God.

As a result, no matter how much effort religious communities devote to making a place for God, no matter what we believe or how we worship, God will not, and cannot, fit in. Indeed, as the Torah notes, when Moses finishes setting up the Tabernacle, "Moses could not enter the Tent of Meeting, because the cloud had settled upon it and the Presence of the LORD filled the Tabernacle" (Exod. 40:24–35). Even in the space designed by God as a place to dwell among the Israelites, when God is too fully present, no human being—not even Moses—can enter. Even there, at the center of Israelite community, God is a stranger who dwells apart.

Although my identification with God helped me recognize God's inherent strangeness, it also represented a kind of private idolatry. Just as the Golden Calf gave the Israelites a deity that fit comfortably into their ideas and lives, my image of God's incurable isolation from human community gave me a deity who fit comfortably into mine. I liked imagining God as being as hopelessly stranded outside humanity as I was, because I didn't want to be alone and couldn't believe that humanity might have room for someone as different as I was. Accepting isolation and despair seemed far safer to me than risking the kind of rejection and heartbreak

God experiences over and over when God tries to find a place among the Israelites.

But the God I found it comfortable to imagine—a God who, as I did, gives up on finding a place in human community, who sobs or sulks alone in a haze of disembodied difference—is not the God we see in the Torah. The God we see there never gives up on finding a place in human community. Even in the midst of the genocidal rages that lead God to imagine wiping out the Israelites after they make the Golden Calf and refuse to occupy Canaan, God is still determined to try again with a new people descended from Moses. Despite all the heartbreak and recrimination God expresses through the biblical prophets, God never stops believing that human communities can make a place for a God who is incomprehensibly strange and utterly different, a God who cannot fit into human roles and categories, but whose presence, like the cloud and fire that surrounded the Tabernacle, is recognized and embraced at the very heart of our lives—not only our lives as isolated individuals, but the lives we live together.

"How Does It Feel to Be a Problem?": God, Transgender People, and Other Hyper-Minorities

Before my transition, I thought it was impossible to do what God tries to do throughout the Torah: find a place in human community as someone who clearly does not fit in. Now that I live as an openly transgender person, I see that I was wrong. Communities can and do include individuals who are too different to fit established roles and categories. Social scientists call people in that position "hyper-minorities." W. E. B. Du Bois, the great African American sociologist and activist, used a simpler term, saying that his own position as a Harvard-educated African American with a PhD at the turn of the twentieth century made him "a problem":

Between me and the other world there is ever an unasked question: unasked by some through feelings of delicacy; by others through the difficulty of rightly framing it. All, nevertheless, flutter round it. They approach me in a half-hesitant sort of way, eye me curiously or compassionately, and then, instead of saying directly, How does it feel to be a problem? they say, I know an excellent colored man in my town; or, I fought at Mechanicsville; or, Do not these Southern outrages make your blood boil? At these I smile, or am interested, or reduce the boiling to a simmer, as the occasion may require. To the real question, How does it feel to be a problem? I answer seldom a word.[4]

Like God among the Israelites, Du Bois here is surrounded by a society—a white society—to which he can never belong. The people who belong to that society can see that Du Bois is different not only from them but also from anyone they know, different in ways that make it impossible for them to understand him, because he doesn't fit the roles and categories assigned to people of color by the brutal early-twentieth-century version of America's racial binary. They don't want to be unfriendly, insult, or otherwise spurn him, but they know that they don't understand how Du Bois sees himself or them or the society they do and do not share. His difference is impossible to ignore and impossible for them to comprehend, a center of attention that not only makes it hard to relate to him but disrupts their usual ways of relating to one another. That makes Du Bois, to them, a problem.[5]

Unlike the well-meaning white people Du Bois portrays who don't know how to relate to someone like him, the Israelites, after the building of the Tabernacle and the establishment of the laws of sacrifice and other rituals, do have defined ways of relating to God. But the sacrificial laws only tell the Israelites how to relate to God in certain situations, such as when they seek forgiveness or want to express gratitude. Those laws and rituals don't tell them how to act in less formal situations, but God is always there, dwelling in their midst—and as we see when the Israelites complain about the monotony of their diet in Numbers 11, the Israelites' inability to understand how God feels about how they talk among themselves can damage their relationship with God:

The riffraff in [the Israelites'] midst felt a gluttonous craving; and then the Israelites wept and said, "If only we had meat to eat! We remember the fish that we used to eat free in Egypt, the cucumbers, the melons, the leeks, the onions, and the garlic. Now our gullets are shriveled. There is nothing at all! Nothing but this manna to look to!"

[The LORD told Moses to say to the Israelites,] "[Y]ou have rejected the LORD who is among you, by whining before [God] and saying, 'Oh, why did we ever leave Egypt!'" (Num. 11:4–6, 20)

The Torah clearly disapproves of the Israelites' complaining, calling those who start it "riffraff" and referring to their desire for a varied diet after months of eating manna for every meal as a "gluttonous craving." But there is no indication that the Israelites mean those complaints as a rejection of God. Grumbling about food is a normal activity in any community that shares the same diet, whether they are Israelites in the wilderness or students on a college campus. To the Israelites, their nostalgia for Egypt is a way of expressing how unhappy they have become with eating only manna—so unhappy that they think back fondly to the time when they had a varied diet, even though that was a time when they were slaves. God takes their complaints not as an expression of dissatisfaction with a diet that never changes but as an expression of dissatisfaction with the God who led them out of Egypt—an interpretation that has fatal consequences, since God responds by striking the Israelites with a plague. To white people, Du Bois is a problem they don't know what to do with; to the Israelites, God is a problem who may at any moment do something to them (Num. 11:20, 33).

Now that I live as myself, I often feel like a problem. I live in communities where I am the only one who is different in the way I am different, the only person who doesn't fit or make sense in what Du Bois would call "the other world" of binary gender. Like Du Bois among white Northerners, I have a place in that "other world," or rather, I have places in a few of the communities that, though otherwise quite unlike one another, are part of the world of binary gender: I have tenure at my Orthodox university, have membership in my non-Orthodox synagogue, and have lived in the same small-town New England area for the past fifteen years. Like Du Bois, I know how it feels to be treated by those around me as too different to fit in: as someone they don't want to exclude but can't understand, someone whose feelings, they fear, might be unintentionally hurt by what, to them, is their normal way of relating to one another. They are always polite, and often kind. No one tells me that they know, and know that I know, that in terms of binary gender, I am a problem.[6]

How does it feel to be a problem? As Du Bois suggests, it can feel lonely, awkward, and uncomfortable. In a later passage describing growing up as a hyper-minority, he talks about feeling "shut out from [others'] world by a vast veil."[7] Being seen as too different to understand by those we dwell among can also make us feel frustrated, overlooked, unappreciated, disregarded, deliberately spurned, despairing, and sometimes very angry. When we express those feelings, which tend to seem inexplicable to those around us, we become even more of a problem.

But to me, being seen as a problem by a community that acknowledges and makes a place, however uncomfortable, for my difference, feels better than believing, as I used to believe, that I had to choose between concealing who I was and being exiled forever—a devastating choice that many transgender people still face. God's persistence in dwelling among the Israelites suggests that God makes a similar decision: God prefers to be seen as a problem—to be recognized as a being the Israelites cannot understand—than not to be seen at all.

Like me and many people who are so different from others in our communities that we are seen as problems, Du Bois portrays himself as treading carefully when negotiating the ways people from the other world respond, and fail to respond, to him.[8] He does not insist that the white people talking about their race-related feelings and experiences listen to his. He says nothing about what it is like to be black in America or to be seen as a problem by them. He has a place among them, but it is a tenuous place, a bubble defined by difference and maintained by silence. He isn't sure, or perhaps is all too sure, whether he would still have a place among them if he spoke his mind.

I find myself behaving similarly at my university. I do not hide my difference—everyone knows that I'm trans—but I never talk about it either. If others say nothing about it, I say nothing. If someone says they know an excellent transgender person, I smile; if they tell me they participated in some action to support LGBTQ rights, I show interest and encouragement; if they express anger at the university's hostility to LGBTQ people, I, like Du Bois, try to reduce the boiling to a simmer. No one ever asks, and I never say, how it feels to be a problem. I accept whatever signs I am given that others recognize my presence among them without expecting or demanding that others accommodate, or even hear about, the feelings and experiences that go with being different in the ways that I am different. Like many people in the position of being hyper-minorities, I fear that if I burst the bubble of silence—if I turn the problem I am into a problem others have to reckon with—then I will no longer have a place in my community.

Needless to say, God in the Torah is not willing to settle for dwelling among the Israelites in silence. When the Israelites act in ways that do not acknowledge God's presence, respect God's concerns, or affirm God's importance to the community, God makes sure that God's problems become the Israelites' problems. Many people in the position of being hyper-minorities keep our anger to ourselves, choosing either to hide our feelings or to leave the community whose failure of understanding has hurt us. God not only expresses God's anger but also demands that the Israelites change their lives to accommodate God.[9]

As far as God and the Torah are concerned, God is a problem that is easily solved: everyone should always accommodate God, no matter how strange or burdensome God's demands may seem.[10] However, as God finds in the Torah, communities can find it hard to accommodate hyper-minorities, particularly when those accommodations require them to do things that do not make sense to them.[11]

For example, take the Israelites' refusal to invade the land of Canaan after they hear the report of the spies God orders be sent to scout out the land (Num. 13:1–3, 13:31–33, 14:2–4). Ten of the twelve spies, all respected leaders of the community, insist that the Canaanites are too strong for the Israelites to overcome, and the Israelites believe them. To God, the Israelites' refusal seems like a denial of God's presence, power, and place in their history and community, a sign that they "have no faith in Me despite all the signs that I have performed in their midst" (Num. 14:11). To the Israelites, recently freed slaves who have no military training, weapons, or equipment, God's insistence that they invade a heavily armed, well-fortified land of walled cities ruled, according to the spies' reports, by giants, seems like God is asking them to commit collective suicide. They refuse to accommodate God's plan because to them, that plan, like God, simply doesn't make sense.

That is a dramatic, onetime confrontation, but as we see from God's response to the Israelites' complaints about their diets, God also expects the Israelites to accommodate God by changing their basic human habits and happily eating a single food, manna, for every meal, day after day, week after week, and year after year. It's not surprising that the Israelites would grow tired of this monotonous diet (the Torah tells us that no matter how it was prepared, manna "tasted like rich cream" [Num. 11:8]), or that they would vent their dissatisfaction by complaining. Indeed, the Israelites have been complaining about their living conditions in the wilderness since they crossed the Red Sea. But to God, what to the Israelites is business as usual—grumbling, wanting a varied diet, avoiding military confrontation with vastly superior forces—seems like rejection, and what seems to God like basic acknowledgment of God's presence and blessings feels to the Israelites like an unreasonable demand that they upend their tastes, their habits, and even their sense of right (protecting their children) and wrong (attacking giant, heavily armed Canaanites).

The Israelites' difficulties in accommodating God may seem familiar to traditional religious communities struggling with how to accommodate openly transgender members.[12] Like people who are openly trans, God refuses to conform to the community's ideas of what God should do or be, and insists that the community change to accommodate God's differences. And like God among the Israelites, openly trans people expect to be recognized no matter how we appear, to be treated with respect no matter how disruptive our presence may seem, and for our feelings to be acknowledged and accommodated, no matter how unusual, hard to understand, or inconvenient they may seem to others in the community.

Because people who are hyper-minorities are by definition different in ways communities find hard to understand, it can be hard for others to anticipate and respond to our feelings, and it is easy for us to feel rejected when they do not. For example, the rabbi of the progressive Jewish community to which I belonged before, during, and after my gender transition didn't understand why I was angry when I learned that he planned to call my daughter to the Torah at her bat mitzvah using my old male Hebrew name, rather than the name I took when I began living as myself.[13] To the rabbi, calling my daughter using my male name was simply a matter of custom; he called all children to the Torah using the names their parents had when they were born. But to me, using my male name when calling my daughter to the Torah would amount to a public rejection of my identity, an announcement that, as far as the rabbi and the congregation were concerned, I was and always would be a man.

The rabbi didn't mean to reject me by calling my daughter to the Torah by my former male name any more than the Israelites meant to reject God by complaining about manna. But it was hard for me not to feel rejected when the rabbi made it clear that he and the community would prefer to follow their usual practices without worrying about how I felt about them, and to go ahead with my daughter's bat mitzvah as though I weren't there.

Like most people, I live on both sides of this situation. In some communities, I am the disregarded, misunderstood minority who is seen as a problem, while in others, I am part of the majority who does not understand the feelings of those who do not fit in. At my university, I am both at once: in the majority, as a relatively able-bodied white person of Ashkenazi Jewish descent, and, as an openly transgender person, the only one of my kind.

Living as myself has not only taught me what it is like to be a hyper-minority; it has also taught me that the experience of being incomprehensibly different is one of the things most people have in common. Whether we are the only openly transgender person in an Orthodox Jewish university, the only black Jew in an otherwise white synagogue, the only white member of a black church, the first blind member of a group in which everyone else can see—no matter who or what we are, we each may find ourselves in the position of being problematic hyper-minorities in some communities, no matter how well we fit into others.

To the extent that God's difficulties dwelling among the Israelites reflect the common difficulties hyper-minorities face, this means that most of us have something in common with God. At some time in our lives, we too have felt invisible and incomprehensible to those we live with and love, and felt rejected by words and actions that, to most members of the community, are simply routine. We too have had to choose between withdrawing from communities that do not understand us, or staying and being a problem.

Of course, the Israelites are dependent on God in a way that other communities are not dependent on human hyper-minorities. Unlike human hyper-minorities, God literally creates and maintains the Israelite community, and even, as we see in the laws of the first Passover, defines what it means to be an Israelite. When, after the incident of the Golden Calf, God threatens to withdraw from the community, the Israelites go into mourning; as difficult as God is to accommodate, they are God's people, and God gives them direction and purpose. By contrast, when human hyper-minorities withdraw, our communities rarely mourn. The problems we were are solved. There is no longer a need to accommodate our differences or think about our feelings, and because our qualities and contributions tend not to be noticed or valued, few lament what they lose when we are not there.

But however problematic God's position among the Israelites may be, the relationship between God and Israel portrayed in the Hebrew Bible makes it clear that both God and the Torah reject my long-held belief that human communities cannot make a place for those who are seen as too different to fit in. No matter how often the Israelites fall short, God continues to dwell among them. And despite the trouble the Israelites have in understanding and accommodating God's differences, they still give, and risk their lives to give, God a place among them.

Knowing the Soul of the Stranger

"You shall not oppress a stranger, for you know the [soul] of the stranger, having yourselves been strangers in the land of Egypt." (Exod. 23:9)[14]

Thinking of God as a hyper-minority has helped me move beyond my childhood assumption that because God is too different to fit into human communities, God cannot have any place among them. It has also helped me see that the conflicts between God and the Israelites in the wilderness do not reflect the Israelites' rejection of God. The Israelites' failures to anticipate and accommodate God's feelings only happen because the Israelites, after the incident of the Golden Calf, dedicate themselves to making a place for a God they know they cannot understand.

But though the hyper-minority model offers a pragmatic way of understanding why the Israelites' relationship with God goes wrong, when it comes to thinking positively about how human communities can make a place for God, it does not get us very far. As I and many others who have lived as hyper-minorities have found, communities tend to treat those who are seen as too different to fit in not just as strange, but as strangers. We have a place in the community, but the place we are given is defined by our differences from other members. Even in communities in which our differences are accommodated, those differences tend to remain the focus of the community's attention, the first and sometimes only thing about us that people think and talk about. No matter how long we have been part of our communities, we are not seen as one of *us*.

That is how Tzipporah, Moses's wife, seems to be treated by the Israelite community. Tzipporah is not an Israelite by birth. She marries Moses when Moses is living in exile with Tzipporah's family in her native land of Midian. When God orders Moses to return to Egypt to begin the Exodus, Tzipporah goes with him, saving his life along the way by averting God's anger through the world's first, and perhaps only, emergency circumcision. After the Exodus, Tzipporah wanders with the Israelites for decades through the wilderness, sharing their diet of manna, miracles, and misery.

The Torah says little about Tzipporah's place in the Israelite community until, in Numbers, Miriam and Aaron, her brother- and sister-in-law, refer to her as "the Cushite woman [Moses] married": "Miriam and Aaron spoke against Moses because of the Cushite woman whom he had married: 'He married a Cushite woman!'" (Num. 12:1). Despite her longstanding connection to the Israelite community and her position as Moses's wife, Tzipporah is not seen as an Israelite but as a member of another people, someone so different that Miriam and Aaron do not hesitate to refer to her solely in terms of her difference.[15] They assume that others, too, think of Tzipporah as nothing but "a Cushite woman," with no other distinguishing personal characteristics, not even a name.

That assumption is particularly revealing of the tendency of communities to treat members who are hyper-minorities as strangers because, as her brother- and sister-in-law certainly know, Tzipporah is a Midianite, not a Cushite.[16] By referring to Tzipporah as a Cushite, her in-laws exaggerate her foreignness (Midianites were part of the ancient Israelites' neighborhood in a way that Cushites were not), and naming Tzipporah solely in terms of her difference makes it seem that to them, and to everyone who accepts this characterization, her difference is all that matters.[17] Tzipporah's history, her complex identity, her character, and her contributions to the community, are irrelevant. No matter how Tzipporah understands herself, no matter how closely she identifies with the Israelite community or what sacrifices she has made to be there, to those whose lives she shares—even to her husband's family—she is a Cushite woman.[18] And though the Torah makes it clear that Miriam and Aaron are wrong for speaking against Moses, their characterization of Tzipporah is accepted by everyone in the scene that follows. God speaks up for Moses, but no one, neither God nor Moses, nor the Torah itself, speaks up for Tzipporah, or insists that despite her differences, she be recognized as part of the Israelite community (Num. 12:2–16).

But in the commandment not to oppress the stranger, God offers a different model for how communities should relate to members who are seen as too different to fit in, a model that rejects the idea that there is an unbridgeable gulf between those who are embraced as *us* and those who, like Tzipporah in the scene in Numbers, are treated as *them*: "You shall not oppress a stranger, for you know the soul of the stranger, having yourselves been strangers in the land of Egypt" (Exod. 23:9).

This commandment combines hardheaded realism, the acknowledgment that even Israelites who were oppressed as strangers in the land of Egypt are likely to oppress others when they have a chance, with the idealistic belief that people who enjoy the privilege and power of being *us* can, and will, identify with those who, like Tzipporah, are seen as *them*.

I have thrilled to those words since I first read them as a child. But I had my doubts about the practicality of this commandment. After all, I hid my female gender identification because I was sure that if others knew about it, even my own family would treat me as a stranger, someone they didn't know and didn't want to know. My skepticism that anyone would ever live up to this commandment was reinforced every time someone in my family reacted to a man they saw as "queer," that is, a man who didn't fit their ideas of how men are supposed to look or act. No one ever responded to seeing a man as queer the way the commandment not to oppress the stranger imagines: by affirming that because, as everyone in my family knew, Jewish men have often been mocked for not meeting non-Jewish standards of masculinity, we, as Jews, knew the soul of the queer. Instead, they made it clear that queer men were people we didn't understand and didn't want to have anything to do with.

Of course, the commandment not to oppress the stranger does not order the Israelites to identify with the experience of not fitting gender norms; it commands them to identify with an experience—being oppressed as strangers in Egypt—that all of them at that time (the commandment is given shortly after the Ten Commandments) could remember. But the commandment is not only directed at Israelites who had lived in Egypt: this law also speaks to the future, when Israelites would be settled in their own society in the land of Canaan. By the time the Israelites invade and occupy Canaan, few of them could remember life in Egypt. Most had been born free in the wilderness and grown up in a community in which Israelites were the ruling majority. They had never set foot in Egypt and had never known what it was to be seen as strangers, to be treated as one of *them* instead of one of *us*, by those they dwelt among. To fulfill this commandment, the Israelites of the future (a category I saw as including me) would have to identify not just with those we saw as strangers but also with the experience of Israelites who lived in Egypt long before we were born. How, I wondered, could anyone do that?

I was also puzzled by the fact that even the Israelites who *had* been slaves seem to forget their lives as strangers in the land of Egypt. The only times the Torah portrays the Israelites recalling life in Egypt, as they do when complaining about manna, they remember their old life fondly, like nostalgic exiles. The Israelites had lived in Egypt for many generations before they were enslaved, and in the wilderness they miss their old lives. Their nostalgia suggests that even when they were enslaved, the Israelites hadn't seen themselves as strangers; no matter how they were treated by the Egyptians, to them, Egypt was home.

That—the experience of being treated as strangers in the society they felt to be their own—is what God orders the Israelites to recall in the commandment not to oppress the stranger. That is what *ger*, the Hebrew word translated as "stranger" in this commandment, means: not someone who is a foreigner, with no permanent ties to Israelite society (the Torah has a different term, *ben*-nachar, for the foreigner), but what U.S. immigration law calls a "resident alien," and the Torah often refers to as "the stranger [*ger*] who dwells among you," a person who, like Tzipporah, lives in and is part of the Israelite community but is seen as too different to be considered one of us.[19]

The Israelites in Egypt officially become *gerim*, resident aliens, when Pharaoh, at the beginning of the book of Exodus, declares that Israelites who have lived in Egypt for generations are not members of Egyptian society but a threat to it: "Look, the Israelite people are much too numerous for us. Let us deal shrewdly with them, so that they may not increase; otherwise in the event of war they may join our enemies in fighting against us" (Exod. 1:10). As Pharaoh makes clear, the Israelites are now to be treated as "them" rather than "us" by the Egyptians they dwell among.[20]

God not only commands the Israelites to keep alive the memory of being treated as strangers by their fellow Egyptians; throughout the laws establishing Israelite rituals and festivals, God also reminds the Israelites to include the stranger. In fact, from the outset, *gerim* are built into God's idea of community and religion. Shortly after the killing of the firstborn and before the parting of the Red Sea, God commands the Israelites to include strangers in the Passover sacrifice, as we saw in the discussion of the laws of the first Passover in chapter 4:[21] "The LORD said to Moses and Aaron: 'This is the law of the Passover offering: No foreigner [*ben-nachar*] shall eat of it. . . . [But] if a stranger [*ger*] who dwells with you would offer the Passover [sacrifice] to the LORD, all his males must be circumcised; then he shall be admitted to offer it; he shall then be as a citizen of the country'" (Exod. 12:43, 48).

It seems unlikely that Moses and Aaron, still in the midst of escaping Egypt, were thinking about how the Israelites would one day treat minorities they see as strangers. But God is. To God, acknowledging and accommodating *gerim*—non-Israelites who identify with the Israelite community so strongly that they not only want to offer the Passover sacrifice but are also willing to be circumcised to do so—is so important that this is among the first commandments God gives after the Israelites begin to leave Egypt.[22]

Here and elsewhere, God insists that all *gerim* who undergo circumcision be treated equally—as citizens—in terms of ritual and civil law. Later Jewish tradition recognized two different kinds of *gerim*: the *ger toshav*, the stranger who lives with you, who commits to observing some but not all of the commandments Israelites are obligated to observe; and the *ger tzedek*, or "righteous stranger," who not only lives in and follows the laws of the community of Israel but also identifies as a Jew and formally converts to Judaism. Rabbinic law requires that communities treat those who convert to Judaism as Jews, and tries to protect them from discrimination by, for example, forbidding other Jews to refer to the fact that a *ger tzedek* was not born Jewish.[23] But, as the term *ger tzedek* shows, no matter how strongly those who are not born Jewish identify as Jews, no matter how fully they embrace Judaism and Jewishness, and no matter how much they have sacrificed to join the Jewish people, the rabbis assume that they will always be seen as *gerim*, strangers.[24] In fact, the Hebrew word for converting to Judaism is *l'hitgayer*, which literally means "to make oneself a stranger": to become a Jew when you are not born a Jew is to identify yourself with a community in which you will always be considered a stranger.[25]

Converting to Judaism is far from the only way people *hitgayer*, estrange ourselves from communities we consider our own. Immigrants make strangers of themselves when they leave their native lands and start new lives in countries where their accents and origins will always mark them as different from those who are born there, and I made a stranger of myself when I stopped living as a man and started living as a woman who is openly transgender.

Of course, even before my transition, I always *felt* like a stranger, because I always knew I didn't fit into a world where everyone had to be either and only male or female. But feeling different didn't make me what the Torah and the rabbis call a *ger*, because the people I dwelt among, the family and communities I considered mine, didn't see me as different. As far as they were concerned, I was one of *us*, a heterosexual male, with all the privileges accorded to people who fit into those categories. To me, living as a male was the opposite of privilege: it was a form of enslavement I endured in order to avoid exile and oppression. But miserable as I was about living as a male, I still received the benefits that went with it. When I was a child, my mother cleaned up for me; she expected my sister to clean up for herself.

When I grew up, I took it for granted that I would be listened to when I spoke up in synagogue or meetings, and that I could walk alone down the darkest, emptiest streets without fear of being raped. As someone seen as a heterosexual man, I never hesitated to hold hands with or kiss a woman in public—things my wife and I now only do when we are sure we are safe. When, in 1982, my now ex-wife and I decided to get married, we knew we could walk into any city hall and get a marriage license. I never worried, as I have since my transition, that my status as a spouse or a parent would be questioned. The IRS gave me tax deductions; my employer automatically included my wife and children in our health insurance; and when my children or my wife were in the hospital, I had the unquestioned right to see them, day or night. My kids never worried about being teased or bullied if their friends found out that I was their parent; they were proud to be known as my children.[26]

In short, before my transition, even though I lived my life in fear of others finding out that I was different, I wasn't seen or treated as a *ger*. But when I began living as myself, I experienced what it means to *hitgayer*, to make oneself a stranger. Members of my family, my university, my synagogue, my small-town community who, when I was a man, had considered me one of them, now saw me as someone they didn't know or understand. People who had always greeted me on the street or at synagogue walked by without a sign of recognition. They weren't trying to slight me. They had known me as a man. Now I was a stranger.

But *ger* and *l'hitgayer* do not refer to the kind of sudden estrangement I experienced as a result of gender transition. They refer to the long-term social situation of living in a community in which, like Tzipporah among the Israelites, no matter how long or how well we are known, we are always seen as too different to fully fit in or be considered one of us. After the shock of transition wears off, that is the position I and many openly transgender people find ourselves in, and that is the position that the rabbis expect people who convert to Judaism to face in Jewish communities. The price for living as who we truly are is that we are seen as *gerim*, strangers, perhaps as righteous strangers, admired for our courage, honesty, and commitment, but strangers nonetheless.[27]

But God makes clear in the laws of Passover and throughout the Torah that though they are seen as strangers, *gerim* are part of the Israelite community. For example, the laws regarding the rituals for absolving the Israelite community leave no doubt that *gerim* too are stained by communal sins: "The whole Israelite community and the stranger residing among them shall be forgiven, for it happened to the entire people through error" (Num. 15:26). Such laws show both that God considers *gerim* part of the Israelite people and that God knows the Israelites must be constantly reminded that their community includes those they see as strangers. Indeed, God repeatedly tells the Israelites that "[t]here shall be one law for you and for the resident stranger . . . You and the stranger shall be alike before the LORD; the same ritual and the same rule shall apply to you and the stranger who resides among you" (Num. 15:15–16).

But in the commandment not to oppress the stranger, God goes beyond reminding the Israelites to acknowledge and include the strangers who dwell among them. Although God does not use the term *hitgayer*, that commandment effectively requires every Israelite to identify as strangers, both collectively, as members of a people who were treated as strangers, and individually, by acknowledging that they know the soul, the experience, of being a stranger.

This commandment does not presume or require that we know how any individual stranger feels. For that, we would have to get to know those we see as strangers as individuals, and God does not, here or elsewhere, command the Israelites to do that. Rather, God commands that we respond to seeing someone as a stranger by remembering the ways in which we too have felt or been seen as too strange to fit in with communities we consider our own.

How can those who have always fit in with those around them know—how can God insist they know, and why does it matter so much to God that they know—the soul of those who are seen as *them*? When I was growing up, I was sure that God and I were the only strangers in a world of human beings who fit in and identified with one another—human beings who would not, and could not, understand or identify with strangers like us. I know now how wrong I was. Few people identify as transgender, but most of us are aware of being different in ways that might be hard for other members of our communities to understand or accept. No one perfectly fits the roles our communities assign us, or the categories that define who is *us* and who is *them*. Each of us is made in the image of the God who does not fit human categories or roles. All of us, like God, dwell among and love those who cannot fully know or understand us. And even those of us who, right now, fit our roles and communities, know that we will change: that we, like God, are not only what we seem to be right now, but are also what we will be. God's assumption is right: because the sense of being different is part of being human, whether or not we have had the experience of being treated as *gerim*, we all know—and, whether or not we wish to admit it, we all have—the soul of the stranger.

Those of us who are hyper-minorities in religious communities don't need to dredge up painful memories of feeling different, steep ourselves in histories of times when our communities were oppressed, or engage in other psychological or spiritual work to know the soul of the stranger. Being seen as different from those among whom we dwell is the price we pay for belonging to our communities. Like the non-Israelites who, as God anticipates during the Exodus, willingly circumcise themselves and all the males in their households to participate in the Passover offering, we willingly, if not happily, *hitgayer*, accept the pain of being seen as strangers in our communities, because to us, those communities are home. But even though we are hyper-minorities, we too need to do the work of identifying with others *we* see as different—by recognizing the kinship between our souls and the souls of those who, to us, are strangers.

Whatever the differences that set hyper-minorities apart, our differences are dwarfed by what we have in common with others in our communities. Our needs are human needs; our loneliness is human loneliness; our love is human love. We can form friendships, serve on committees, greet people at the door, study sacred texts, dance at weddings, hold mourners in our arms, raise our voices in song. And so, however hard our differences may be for our communities to reckon with, we will always be easier to include than God. Our differences from other people, as Maimonides might say, are differences of degree; God's differences are absolute.

God is not just a stranger in this or that community: God is the ultimate *ger*, a singular Presence who, as Judaism and other traditions that grew out of the Torah teach, dwells among human beings, sharing our lives, caring about our actions, knowing our sorrows and our struggles, but who can never fit in or be seen as one of us. That perhaps is why God worries about making a place for the *ger* even while the Israelites are still leaving Egypt: because to make a place for God, the Israelites, and the other religious communities that have grown out of the Torah, must make a place for a stranger who dwells among them.

From this perspective, the commandment to know the soul of the stranger is more than a summons to social justice or a reminder not to do to others the evil that others have done to us. Knowing the soul of the stranger is part of the spiritual discipline required for a community to make a place for God. In the Torah, God constantly prompts the Israelites to practice this spiritual discipline. God institutes rituals, like that of Passover, that keep the memory of being strangers in Egypt alive and central to Israelite identity; God gives laws that demand that those who are seen as strangers be treated equally and included fully in communal life; and God commands the Israelites to *hitgayer*, to identify with the experience of being strangers so that they know the soul of the stranger—the stranger who dwells among them, the strangers they are, the stranger who is God.

Although these laws are specific to the Israelites, the spiritual discipline they represent is not. Regardless of our religious tradition or affiliation, to welcome God into our communities is to welcome a stranger who will never assimilate, who will not go along to get along, who will not follow our rules, accept our judgments, embrace our values, affirm our doctrines, confirm our biases, or look or behave the way we expect—a stranger who may bless us or curse us, who is responsible for all the good and all the evil that befalls us, who takes without asking and gives without explanation. To love God, we must learn to love someone who will always be a stranger. To serve God, we must serve the needs of a stranger. To grow close to God, we must become intimate with a stranger. To open ourselves to God, we must open ourselves to a stranger. To make a place for the God who dwells invisibly and incomprehensibly among us—to show that God belongs with us, and that we belong to God—we must know, and build our lives and communities around knowing, the soul of the stranger.

NOTES

INTRODUCTION *Shipwrecked with God*

1. I am building here on Judith Plaskow's argument for feminist theology, particularly her insistence that redefining humanity to be more gender inclusive "demands a new understanding of God that reflects and supports [that] redefinition" (231). Plaskow is discussing the theological consequences of recognizing the humanity of women, but I believe her argument also holds when it comes to recognizing the humanity of trans people, not only because we need theology to "reflect and support" inclusion of women and transgender people, but also because every time we expand our understanding of what it means to be human, we create the potential for expanding our understanding of God. See Judith Plaskow, "The Right Question Is Theological," in *On Being a Jewish Feminist*, ed. Susannah Heschel, 223–233 (New York: Schocken, 1995).

2. I pay particular attention to how analogies to transgender experience can help us think about God in chapters 3 and 5.

3. Some transsexuals object to being considered "transgender," either because, unlike other transgender people, they identify themselves as men or women, or because they feel that being transsexual involves feelings and experiences that are not shared by other transgender people. I certainly understand those concerns. For me, "transsexual" is a term that specifically, though clinically, describes the relationship to gender and identity that has so profoundly shaped my life, while "transgender" is a term that helps me recognize what I have in common with others who do not fit binary gender categories. Similarly, I embrace "Jewish" as a general term that expresses my sense of identification with Jews across history and around the world, even though it does not indicate my specific relation to Jewishness and Judaism.

4. Barry Holtz, ed., *Back to the Sources: Reading the Classic Jewish Texts* (New York: Simon & Schuster, 1985), 185.

5. Rabbi Dr. Burton Visotzky, professor of midrash at the Jewish Theological Society, pointed out to me that in connecting the Torah's portrayals of God to my human experiences, I am offering a contemporary example of the Talmudic practice of *mashal l'melech basar v'dam*, literally "like a king of flesh and blood," in which aspects of the divine are explained through analogies to the behavior of human kings.

6. Nonreligious and religious but nontraditional communities also often find it hard to include openly transgender people, because their customs, roles, and ways of relating to one another are also based on gender binary assumptions.

ONE *The Genesis of Gender*

1. Although the definitions of male and female characteristics and roles vary widely, I am not aware of any culture that does not divide and define individuals, family relationships, and social roles in terms of binary gender. Even though some cultures provide for what are often called "third genders," the vast majority of people are defined in terms of the local version of male or female.

2. As Judith Butler demonstrates in the first chapter of *Gender Trouble*, even the most penetrating, sophisticated, and revolutionary critiques of gender tend to rely on and reinforce binary gender categories. See Judith Butler, *Gender Trouble: Feminism and the Subversion of Identity* (New York: Routledge, 1990), 1–34.

3. *Annie Hall*, directed by Woody Allen (Los Angeles, CA: United Artists, 1977).

4. Noach Dzmura provides an excellent, practical discussion of the rabbinic laws regarding intersex Jews. See Noach Dzmura, "An Ancient Strategy for Managing Gender Ambiguity," in *Balancing on the Mechitza: Transgender in the Jewish Community*, ed. Noach Dzmura, 170–181 (Berkeley, CA: North Atlantic Books, 2010).

5. The Hebrew word I am translating as "humanity" is *adam*. *Adam* means "earth," "man," and humanity in general, and, as I will discuss below, becomes the first man's name. But this translation smooths over a complication: as rabbinic readers noticed, Genesis 1:27 can be read as saying

that God created *adam*, the first human being, both male and female, as an androgyne. (See, for example, Genesis Rabbah 8:1–2.) If we read the verse this way, the first chapter of Genesis not only fails to mention gender but also presents humanity as being created without the division into male and female on which binary gender is based.

6. See, for example, the Ikar Siftei Hachamim on verse 4: "[A]ccording to the simple understanding of the text, it is implied that at first they [light and darkness] were mixed together as one" (Ikar Siftei Hachamim Gen. 1:4). Similarly, Rashi explains God's division of light from darkness by saying, "[God] saw that [the light] was good, and that it was not seemly that light and darkness should function together in a confused manner" (Rashi Gen. 1:4 [DH—And God saw]).

7. Throughout this book, unless otherwise noted, English translations of the Hebrew Bible come from *Tanakh, The Holy Scriptures: The New JPS Translation According to the Traditional Hebrew Text*. Philadelphia: Jewish Publication Society, 1985.

8. Joanne Meyerowitz, *How Sex Changed: A History of Transsexuality in the United States* (Cambridge, MA: Harvard University Press, 2002), 23.

9. Of course, as the Talmud acknowledged, and as the rabbis acknowledged with such categories as the "androgynose," seen above in Genesis Rabbah 8:1, some human bodies don't fit male and female norms, though this fact is obscured by modern medicine's penchant for surgically "correcting" the genitals of intersex newborns, a Western form of genital mutilation that attests to our profound, sometimes violent determination to make reality fit binary categories.

10. Although I developed my reading years before I came across Phyllis Trible's groundbreaking work, this reading of what I call the genesis of gender has striking parallels to Trible's efforts to "depatriarchalize" Genesis's account of the creation of humanity. While Trible's focus is different than mine (her concern is showing that this account should not be read as implying that God created men to be dominant and women to be subordinate), her reading and mine agree on several key points, particularly the idea that gender as we know it emerges gradually in chapters 2 and 3, and that patriarchy—a binary gender system based on male dominance—is portrayed as a divine curse (punishment for eating the fruit of the Tree

of the Knowledge of Good and Evil) rather than as a built-in feature of humanity. See "Depatriarchalizing in Biblical Interpretation," *Journal of the American Academy of Religion* 41, no. 1 (March 1973): 30–48; and "Eve and Adam: Genesis 2–3 Reread," in *Womanspirit Rising: A Feminist Reader in Religion*, ed. Carol P. Christ and Judith Plaskow, 74–83 (San Francisco: HarperSanFrancisco, 1992).

11. Although this verse doesn't say "husband," it is implied by the term "wife" (literally, "his woman"), because a heterosexual man (the only kind envisioned here) cannot have a wife without being a husband (that is, without being his woman's man).

12. "Depatriarchalizing in Biblical Interpretation," 38.

13. According to the curse, and to many definitions of male social roles, Adam has to work for bread whether he wants to or not—and Adam, like many men, clearly doesn't want to do the work he is now required to do. If he did want to, God wouldn't assign that work as punishment.

14. See Kate Bornstein, *Gender Outlaw: On Men, Women, and the Rest of Us* (New York: Vintage, 1995).

15. Jewish tradition has interpreted the first-person plural as implying that God is declaring God's intentions to an angelic court, but however we read it, it is clear that God's intentions focus on the resemblance between humanity and divinity rather than on the sex of human bodies. See, for example, the arguments for and against the creation of humanity in Genesis Rabbah 8:5.

TWO *Trans Experience in the Torah*

1. The Hebrew name of the Book of Numbers, *Bamidbar*, means "In the Wilderness."

2. As the example of adolescence suggests, our gender roles are often bound up with other aspects of our lives, such as our age, or economic class. Old women are assigned different roles than young women; working-class men are expected to play roles that are very different from those of men born to wealth. Even when we broadly agree about the gender binary distinction between male and female, the roles we are assigned and expected

to play as men and women vary widely from one culture, economic class, place, time, and even family to another.

3. The importance placed on determining which son is the firstborn is highlighted in the story of the birth of Tamar's twin sons: "While [Tamar] was in labor, one of [the twins] put out his hand, and the midwife tied a crimson thread on that hand, to signify: This one came out first. But just then he drew back his hand, and out came his brother" (Gen. 38:28–29).

4. I discuss Ishmael and Isaac's troubled history as Abraham's sons in the last section of this chapter.

5. As I explained in the introduction, transsexuals are transgender people who, like me, are born into one gender but identify as the opposite gender.

6. As Talia Bettcher and others have noted, one of the transphobic stereotypes of transgender people is that we are "deceivers," using gender signs, like Jacob, to manipulate others by fooling them into thinking we are someone other than we are. See, for example, Talia Bettcher, "Evil Deceivers and Make-Believers: On Transphobic Violence and the Politics of Illusion," *Hypatia* 22, no. 3 (Summer 2007): 43–65.

7. I describe my childhood identification with Jacob in my memoir of gender transition, *Through the Door of Life: A Jewish Journey Between Genders* (Madison, WI: University of Wisconsin Press, 2012), 115–117.

8. As gender theorists would say, in this scene, the Torah presents gender as performance rather than essence, as something Jacob *does* that causes his father to interpret his gender as being like his brother's rather than what Jacob *is*.

9. Although persistent gender dysphoria is usually thought of as something transgender people experience, as I am suggesting here, non-trans people may also experience gender dysphoria, at least in passing.

10. Isaac's reliance on gender not only prevents him from recognizing his own son; it even prevents him, a man who has spent his entire life among flocks and herds, from recognizing the difference between animal and human hair and skin.

11. See, for example, Genesis Rabbah 38:13, which imagines the young Abraham smashing his father's idols.

12. Of course, no one outside Abraham's household would understand

this new identity unless Abraham explained it. Having gone through my own hard-to-explain change in name and social role, it's easy for me to imagine the awkwardness of Abraham's conversations with those who had known him before his circumcision: "Peace be with you, Abram." "Peace be with you—but actually, my name is Abraham now." "Oh, why is that?" "Well, the creator of Heaven and Earth told me to take a flint knife and cut off—never mind. Please just call me Abraham."

13. Jacob's wives, Leah and Rachel, engage in this practice early in their marriage, and Leah does so even though she has already had children of her own (Gen. 30:1–12).

14. Although the Torah does not describe it, Hagar presumably endures her own form of trans experience, simultaneously occupying the conflicting roles of despised slave and mother of the patriarch's heir.

15. By contrast, when Rachel, wife of Sarah's grandson Jacob, responds to her own fertility problems by giving her maid to her husband, she embraces the sons born to her servant Bilhah as her own (Gen. 30:4–8).

16. Because Hagar, at God's behest, returns from the wilderness and endures Sarah's harsh treatment, Ishmael grows up as Abraham's firstborn and is circumcised before his brother Isaac is conceived. Although Sarah drives Hagar and Ishmael out into the wilderness so that her son Isaac can become Abraham's undisputed heir, God passes on to Ishmael the Abrahamic blessing of becoming the father of "a great nation" (Gen. 21:18). When Hagar runs away, an angel assures Hagar that God "will greatly increase your offspring, / And they shall be too many to count" (Gen. 16:9). When God promises Abraham an heir through Sarah, God responds to Abraham's prayer on behalf of Ishmael by saying, "I hereby bless him. I will make him fertile and exceedingly numerous . . . and I will make of him a great nation" (Gen. 17:20), a promise God repeats to Hagar when she and her son are driven out into the wilderness after Isaac is weaned (21:18).

17. The rabbis use the term *ayolonit*, which some have understood as an individual assigned female at birth but lacking secondary sex characteristics such as breasts, and unable to bear children. See Talmud Bavli Yevamot 64b. Translations from the Talmud are based on *Soncino Babylonian Talmud*, trans. Maurice Simon (London: Soncino Press, 1990).

18. Another commentator, Rabbi Ammi, says that neither Sarah nor

her husband had recognizably male or female genitalia—that they were both what we would now call intersex (Talmud Bavli Yevamot 64a). Trans Jews seeking to find room in Jewish tradition for those who are not simply male or female often point to passages like these, which recognize the existence of intersex Jews. See, for example, Reuven Betzalel Ben Acher, "Lekh Lekha," *Eish Zarah* blog, https://eishzarah.wordpress.com/tag/tumtum.

19. The male-centered narratives of Genesis don't show much of Sarah's relationship with God, but when we contrast her response to her infertility with those of her daughter-in-law Rebekah and granddaughter-in-law Rachel, Sarah's relationship with God becomes clearer. Although Rebekah and Rachel also have trouble conceiving, neither of them attributes her difficulties to God. Moreover, the Torah portrays Rebekah's relief from infertility as reflecting her husband Isaac's relationship with God rather than her own: "Isaac pleaded with the LORD on behalf of his wife, because she was barren; and the LORD responded to his plea, and his wife Rebekah conceived" (Gen. 25:2). Rachel turns not to God but to her husband for help: "Give me children," she says to him, "or I shall die," to which Jacob responds, "Can I take the place of God, who has denied you fruit of the womb?" (Gen. 30:1, 2). Unlike Rebekah and Rachel, Sarah doesn't ask her husband to intercede with God to help her conceive. She simply tells him that God has kept her from bearing, and presents her own plan (forcing Hagar to have sex with him) for working around it.

20. Abraham laughs without fear and God accepts his laughter without comment. But God terrifies Sarah by asking why she laughed, and Sarah responds by denying her laughter. Like many others, I have long wondered why Sarah, in her moment of greatest intimacy with God (at least as recorded in the Torah), lies, particularly when God clearly knows the truth. I don't know, but I do know that concealing and misrepresenting feelings is often part of trans experience. I spent much of my life hiding any feelings connected with my female gender identity. Jacob hides his feelings during his deception of Isaac; Abraham conceals any guilt, remorse, or worry he might have felt in abandoning his father. We know that Sarah felt her gender failure long before she expressed it to Abraham. Perhaps she felt too exposed when God and Abraham glimpsed her feelings after a lifetime of self-restraint, or perhaps, after decades of God ignoring her

obvious misery, she was unable, at least in that moment, to feel safe sharing her feelings with God.

21. Sarah's miraculous conception confounds the gender binary fusion of biology—the physical changes that go with being elderly, the normal reproductive capacity of women—with the social roles of old woman and new mother.

22. In highlighting the ways in which Genesis links trans experience and relationship with God, I do not mean to suggest that God or the Torah, here or elsewhere, undermines either the gender binary or the patriarchal social order. Although Sarah's miraculous pregnancy confounds conventional gender categories, that miracle also reflects and reinforces the idea that women should have children and that wives should give their husbands male heirs. Abraham's violation of patriarchal norms—his abandonment of his elderly father and position as heir, his public circumcision—doesn't stop him from being an extremely successful patriarch; indeed, the Torah parades Abraham's patriarchal successes—his wealth, his social status, his military triumph—as signs of God's blessing and God's presence. But God's association with trans experience in these stories makes it clear that neither God, nor relationships with God, nor the human beings who engage in those relationships, are bound by binary gender categories.

23. If God had not prevented Sarah from bearing children, Ishmael, Isaac's older brother and only sibling, would have either never been born or been born after Isaac and presumably adopted rather than rejected by Sarah.

24. Isaac's attempt to pass his blessing on to his firstborn son is thwarted not just by Rebekah and Jacob but also by God's decree that his younger son would triumph over his older brother.

25. Sarah's rage subjects Ishmael, like his mother Hagar, to forms of trans experience, transforming him overnight from Abraham's firstborn son to an exile with no gender role or status in Abraham's household. The Torah portrays God as approving the horrific treatment of Hagar and Ishmael, but not as directly bringing trans experience upon them.

26. Abraham's distress does not seem to have inspired much compassion toward Hagar and Ishmael. Early in the morning of the day after Sarah

makes her demand, he sends them into the wilderness with nothing but "some bread and a skin of water" (Gen. 21:14).

27. In terms of violating gender roles and values, Abraham's near-sacrifice of Isaac, like his abandonment of his elderly father, represents a form of trans experience. But unlike leaving his father's house, what Abraham does in the Akedah does not make him a different kind of man, because, as his circumcision demonstrated, he has long been a man primarily defined by his relationship with God. The Akedah represents a more extreme version of the form of trans experience that marked the beginning of Abraham's relationship with God, but not a different form, just as the blessings Abraham receives at the end of the Akedah represent more emphatic forms of the blessings God promised him in that first interaction.

28. Of course, gender is not a nightmare for everyone. But as Kate Bornstein emphasizes in *My Gender Workbook*, most people, trans and non-trans alike, sacrifice parts of ourselves on the altar of what gender tells us we should or shouldn't want or do or be. See Kate Bornstein, *My Gender Workbook: How to Become a Real Man, a Real Woman, the Real You, or Something Else Entirely* (New York: Routledge, 1997).

29. Perhaps Abraham's violation of paternal trust contributed to Isaac's later determination to keep faith with Esau, Isaac's favored son, by giving him his innermost blessing. Isaac knew how it felt for a child raised as a firstborn son to be sacrificed for the sake of his father's relationship with God.

30. In Isaac's family, where everyone seems to talk with God, Isaac's silence speaks volumes. Abraham engages in extended dialogues with God; Sarah lies to God about laughing; Rebekah, Isaac's wife, asks God why her pregnancy is so painful (Gen. 25:22); Isaac's son Jacob speaks to God at crucial moments in his roller-coaster career (Gen. 28:22, 32:10–13, 46:2). But the only indication the Torah gives that Isaac ever addresses God is that "Isaac pleaded with the LORD on account of his wife, because she was barren" (Gen. 25:21). We don't know, though, if this refers to formal prayer or a more intimate communication, because the Torah doesn't record a single word spoken by Isaac to God.

31. In a previous footnote, I suggested that God approves but does not

directly impose trans experience on Ishmael, but God is at least indirectly responsible, and Ishmael certainly belongs on the list of family members who leave the gender roles they were born to.

32. As Burton Visotzky writes, the God portrayed in the Torah "is metaethical. . . . For God is not bound, nor does God bind according to the ethical rules of human relationships or society." See Burton Visotzky, *The Genesis of Ethics* (New York: Three Rivers Press, 1996), 62.

33. Genesis Rabbah 56:8.

34. For one of many contemporary *divrei Torah* that present this view, see Rabbi Hyim Shafner, "Did Abraham Fail His Final Test?" Morethodoxy, October 12, 2010, https://morethodoxy.org.

THREE *Close Encounters with an Incomprehensible God*

1. I also talk about this friendship in my memoir, *Through the Door of Life*, 25–26.

2. Plaskow is referring specifically to the fact that when we recognize that Jewish tradition conceives of God in male, patriarchal terms that reflect the idea that only men are fully human, we can see that expanding our definition of humanity to include women creates both the possibility and the need for new ways of conceiving of God. See Plaskow, "The Right Question Is Theological," 231.

3. Moses Maimonides, *Guide for the Perplexed*, Book I, trans. Shlomo Pines (Chicago: University of Chicago Press, 1963), Ch. 35, 42a.

4. Of course, Maimonides would probably not have understood why I felt different, because he shows no sign of questioning binary gender or patriarchy. He not only refers to God with masculine pronouns, but he also assumes and asserts that only men are fit for true metaphysical, philosophical, or spiritual understanding. But this fantasy dialogue imagines a Maimonides who not only understands but also accepts my transgender identity.

5. Actually, *The Guide for the Perplexed* suggests that Maimonides might have felt duty bound to teach me negative theology: "The negation of the doctrine of the corporeality of God and the denial of [God's] having a likeness to created things and of [God's] being subject to affections are

matters that ought to be made clear and explained to everyone according to his capacity and ought to be inculcated in virtue of traditional authority upon children, women, stupid ones, and those of a defective natural disposition, just as they adopt the notion that God is one, that [God] is eternal, and that none but [God] should be worshipped" (*Guide for the Perplexed*, Book I, Ch. 35, 42b).

6. As one of Maimonides's many statements of negative theological principles details: "For [God] does not possess quantity so that there might pertain to [God] a quality pertaining to quantity as such. Nor does [God] receive impressions and affections so that there might pertain to [God] a quality belonging to the affections. Nor does [God] have dispositions so that there might be faculties and similar things pertaining to [God]. Nor is [God] ... endowed with a soul, so that [God] might have a habitus pertaining to [God]—such as clemency, modesty, and similar things—or have pertain to [God] that which pertains to animate beings as such—for instance, health and illness. It is accordingly clear to you that no attribute that may be brought under the supreme genus of quality can subsist in [God]" (*Guide for the Perplexed*, Book I, Ch. 52, 60a).

7. Maimonides argues that even when we say that God exists—a statement Maimonides himself makes, and that many religious martyrs have died to demonstrate—we misrepresent God by suggesting that God shares the quality of existence with, and thus is similar to, other beings: "How ... can a relation be represented between [God] and what is other than [God] when there is no notion comprising in any respect both of the two, inasmuch as [even the term] existence is, in our opinion, affirmed of [God] ... merely by way of absolute equivocation" (*Guide for the Perplexed*, Book I, Ch. 52, 61a).

In saying that we can speak of God sharing the attribute of existence with God's creatures "only by way of absolute equivocation," Maimonides implies that God *can* be represented in human terms, as long as those terms are written and read by people who are sufficiently enlightened (which, to Maimonides, means highly educated men) to understand that these terms are "equivocations" that do not accurately denote God. But he soon dispels that implication. Anticipating what twentieth-century linguists called the Whorf-Sapir hypothesis, which holds that our conception of reality is inescapably shaped by the structure of our language, Maimonides argues that not only the terms but also the very subject-predicate structure of language misrepresents God. (See Book I, Ch. 60.) According to Maimonides, when we make a statement of which God is the subject, such as "God exists," even if we understand the verb "exists" as an "equivocation" that does not imply that God exists in the way that other things exist, and even if we know that God isn't like other subjects and that the predicates we use in connection to God are not like the predicates we use in connection to other subjects, the very representation of God in the subject-predicate form dictated by language betrays the oneness of God by implying that God can be distinguished from God's attributes.

If God is misrepresented by the very structure of human language, then God is literally unspeakable, for to speak of God in any way is to imply that God, like other subjects human beings know and speak of, is describable in terms of attributes and predicates that can be distinguished from and related to the subject. This means that the form of the statement "God is One" implicitly contradicts its content, because it implies that we can distinguish God from God's oneness—and thus implies that God is not, in fact, "One."

8. For example, Maimonides writes: "Thus all philosophers say: We are dazzled by His beauty, and He is hidden from us because of the intensity with which He comes manifest, just as the sun is hidden to eyes that are too weak to apprehend it. This has been expatiated upon in words that it would serve no useful purpose to repeat here. The most apt phrase concerning this subject is the dictum occurring in the Psalms, 'Silence is praise to Thee,' which interpreted signifies: silence with regard to You is praise [Ps. 65:2]. This is a most perfectly put phrase regarding this matter. For of whatever we say intending to magnify and exalt, on the one hand we find that it can have some application to Him, may He be exalted, and on the other we perceive in it some deficiency. Accordingly, silence and limiting oneself to the apprehensions of the intellects are more appropriate—just as the perfect ones have enjoined when they said: 'Commune with your own heart upon your bed and be still' [Ps. 4:4]" (*Guide for the Perplexed*, Book I, Ch. 59, 73a–b).

9. Although Sarah's experience of becoming a mother after a lifetime

of infertility through God's intervention was in many ways parallel to my experience of God enabling me to finally live my female gender identity after a lifetime as a male, I found it hard to relate to her story, because unlike Sarah's, my miracle did not give me the kind of female body I had longed for, a body able to conceive, bear children, and otherwise experience female reproductive powers and pains.

10. Abraham's one effort to understand God in human terms occurs when he talks with God about the judgment of Sodom and Gomorrah, a dialogue I will examine in detail in the next section of this chapter.

11. Although many rabbinic tales portray Abraham as teaching others about God, with one exception, the Torah does not record Abraham saying anything about God. The only time when Abraham breaks his silence is when he explains to the king of Sodom that he has made a vow to "the LORD, the most high God, the possessor of heaven and earth" (Gen. 14:22) not to take spoils of war. The terms Abraham uses in this scene make God visible historically, as someone to whom Abraham has made a vow; politically, as someone whose status is higher and whose claim on Abraham is accordingly greater than that of the king of Sodom; and theologically, as a "higher" deity than any the king of Sodom might worship.

12. Although Sarah later recognizes God in the brief exchange about her laughter, Abraham continues to mistake God for three men until after Abraham, good host that he is, sees the men off, and God becomes present in a way that Abraham can recognize: "The men went on from there to Sodom, while Abraham remained standing before the LORD" (Gen. 18:22).

13. God's self-anthropomorphizing presentations are the social equivalent of what Lurianic Kabbalists call *tzimtzum*, the contraction of the Divine to make space for that which is not divine. (I am indebted to Elizabeth Denlinger, my wife, for suggesting this idea [private communication].) Unlike Lurianic *tzimtzum*, God's self-presentation here has no cosmological or theological implications: it is a purely social form of *tzimtzum*, a relationship-fostering gesture that does not reveal, express, or permanently alter the nature of God.

14. Maimonides might dismiss this scene as an example of the Torah's tendency to represent God in ways that make God seem human. But when the Torah tells us that "the word of the LORD came to Abram in a vision,"

no anthropomorphization is involved. It is not God but God's "word" that comes to Abraham, and even that word comes in a form, a vision, that, like other dream states, suspends the usual human terms of time and space. (In the Torah, only God communicates through visions.) Abraham's matter-of-fact response to this invisible word from beyond, like his earlier responses to God, shows that neither he nor the Torah needs God to appear in anthropomorphic terms. The Torah portrays God as stepping out with Abraham to look at the stars not because it is anthropomorphizing God, but because it is showing how God responds to the human dynamics of God's relationship with Abraham.

15. Although Abraham assumes from the moment God raises the subject that God will destroy Sodom and Gomorrah, God only tells Abraham that God is going to see if the cities are as bad as God has heard.

16. God invites Abraham to participate in the process of judgment through an act of social *tzimtzum*. God presents to Abraham as a being whose knowledge, like a human being's, is limited by space and time, and speaks as though the judgment of Sodom and Gomorrah depends on a fact-finding mission. God's localization in time and space invites and empowers Abraham to weigh in in a way that would not have been possible if God had presented the judgment of Sodom and Gomorrah as yet another revelation of a future that, from God's divine perspective, is already certain.

17. Although God ends the dialogue, Abraham makes it clear that ten people is his last and final offer: "And he said, Let not my LORD be angry if I speak but this last time: What if ten should be found there?"

18. Contrary to Abraham's insistence that it is unlike God to sweep away the innocent with the guilty, the Torah often portrays God as executing judgments, such as the ancient flood that destroys most life on earth, in which innocent and guilty suffer the same fate. Even the destruction of Sodom and Gomorrah includes children who could not justly be considered guilty.

19. This is obviously not the case when we present identities we know are false, as I did when presenting myself as a man.

20. *Mekhilta De-Rabbi Ishmael*, trans. Jacob Z. Lauterbach (New York: Jewish Publication Society, 2010), on Exodus 20:2.

21. Ibid.

22. Yochanan Muffs's *The Personhood of God* offers an excellent survey of the ways God manifests in and is represented by the Torah. See Yochanan Muffs, *The Personhood of God: Biblical Theology, Human Faith and the Divine Image* (Woodstock, VT: Jewish Lights Publishing, 2005).

23. Even though some rabbinic stories portray God's speech at Sinai as being delivered in divine rather than human language, the Torah does not. When God speaks in the first chapter of Genesis, we know that God is speaking in divine language, because God's words have world-creating force. But the words God speaks from Mount Sinai don't change reality. For example, the commandment that "You shall not make for yourself a sculptured image" doesn't prevent idols from being created; a few weeks after God says it, the Israelites are worshipping the Golden Calf. Similarly, even though God's "I am" at Mount Sinai is louder and more memorable than a human being's "I am," when God stops talking, the effectiveness of God's self-identification fades. Forty days after Moses ascends to talk with God, the Israelites no longer seem to perceive God's presence: "When the people saw that Moses was so long in coming down from the mountain, the people gathered against Aaron and said to him, 'Come, make us a god who shall go before us, for that man Moses, who brought us from the land of Egypt—we do not know what has happened to him'" (Exod. 32:1). Not only have the people, still camping at the base of the mountain where they heard God say "I am," forgotten that God is there, despite God's declaration that "I am the LORD your God who brought you out of the land of Egypt," they credit Moses, rather than God, with the Exodus from Egypt. (I discuss this scene in more detail in chapter 5.)

24. In comparing God's ways of presenting to human beings to those of transgender people, I am not suggesting that God "is" transgender. No matter how strange our gender identities or expressions may seem, transgender people are human. Although the sex of our bodies may not express who we are, unlike God, we have bodies that others can see, faces others can recognize, forms that others can touch and love. As Maimonides would tell us, no matter how incomprehensible we may be in terms of binary gender, every transgender person has more in common with non-trans human beings (almost everything) than any human being, trans or not, has in common with God.

25. According to Maimonides, "All the names of God, may He be exalted, are derived except the articulated name [i.e., the Tetragrammaton]"—that is, all names other than YHVH are human terms that identify what God has done or how God has appeared rather than naming God directly. (See *Guide for the Perplexed*, Book I, Ch. 62, 81a.)

26. As a public name for God, Ehyeh-Asher-Ehyeh seems to have been a failure. The Torah does not record a single instance of Moses following God's command to tell the Israelites "*Ehyeh* has sent me to you," presumably because no one would follow a prophet representing a God named "I am" or "I will be." But though it is only mentioned in passing, Ehyeh-Asher-Ehyeh is an important name, because it identifies God in terms that apply to human beings as well as to God.

27. Two commentaries in Exodus Rabbah make this sense of Ehyeh-Asher-Ehyeh explicit: "R. Abba b. Mammel said: 'God said to Moses: "You wish to know My name; I am called according to My deeds. Sometimes I am called 'El Shadday,' 'Tzveo'ot,' 'Elohim,' 'YHVH.' When I judge the creations I am called 'Elohim' [Judge]. When I am waging war against the wicked I am called 'Tzveo'ot' [LORD of Hosts]. When I suspend [punishment] for a man's sins I am called 'El Shadday' [Almighty God]. When I am merciful towards My world, I am called 'YHVH,' for 'YHVH' only refers to the attribute of mercy, as it is said: 'The LORD, the LORD [YHVH, YHVH], God, merciful and gracious.' Hence, 'Ehyeh-Asher-Ehyeh' [I am that I am, or I will be that I will be]—I am called according to My deeds.'" R. Yitzhak said: 'God said to Moses: "Tell them, that I am who was, that I am now, and that I will be in the future." For this reason the word "eheyeh" is written three times.'" (Exodus Rabbah 3:6)

Translations of passages from Exodus Rabbah are based on *Midrash Rabbah*, ed. Harry Freedman and Maurice Simon (London: Soncino Press, 1992).

FOUR *Reading between the Binaries*

1. See W. H. Auden, "In Memory of Sigmund Freud," in *Selected Poems*, ed. Edward Mendelson, 94 (New York: Vintage Books, 1979).

2. I discuss my relation to this law as a child at some length in *Through the Door of Life*, 171–173.

3. For example, Rashi says that the prohibition against women wearing men's clothing is intended to prevent a woman from "look[ing] like a man, in order to consort with men, for this can only be for the purpose of adultery (unchastity)" (cf. Talmud Bavli Nazir 59a). See Rashi on Deuteronomy 22:5 (DH—Neither *shall a man put on a woman's garment*). This translation is based on *The Commentators' Bible: Exodus, Leviticus, Numbers, Deuteronomy: The Rubin JPS Miqra'ot Gedolot*, ed. Michael Carasik (New York: Jewish Publication Society, 2009–2015).

4. This response to the Torah's narrative style was inspired by Erich Auerbach's analysis of that style in the Akedah. See Erich Auerbach, "Odysseus' Scar," in *Mimesis: The Representation of Reality in Western Literature*, trans. Willard R. Trask, 3–23 (Princeton, NJ: Princeton University Press, 1953).

5. While I read the Torah from a Jewish perspective, my intention is to explore how the Torah might speak to transgender concerns that are not specific to Jews.

6. Maimonides explores the implications of this Talmudic concept at length in *Guide for the Perplexed*. See particularly Book I, Chapter 26, which begins, "You know their dictum that refers in inclusive fashion to all the kinds of interpretation connected with this subject [that is, the representation of God in the Torah], namely, their saying: The Torah speaketh in the language of the sons of man." Maimonides is primarily interested in the "language of . . . men" that the Torah uses to represent, and thus to misrepresent, God. However, as I discuss here, the Torah also uses the language of men to represent, and misrepresent, humanity.

7. For one of many analyses of the Torah's male-centered language, see Cynthia Ozick, "Notes Toward Finding the Right Question," in *On Being a Jewish Feminist*, ed. Susannah Heschel, 120–151 (New York: Schocken, 1995).

8. Moses's over-the-top characterization of God's "abhorrence" of those who cross-dress offers one of the few moments in which the Torah enables us to glimpse how this "language of men" in general, and the language of Moses in particular, colors its portrayal of God by identifying God with ancient patriarchal attitudes toward gender.

9. For reasons having nothing to do with transgender lives, Numbers is called *Bamidbar*, or "In the Wilderness," in Hebrew.

10. Because membership in both the tribe of Levi and the Levite clans was passed down through fathers, tribes and clans were also based on the gender binary.

11. Ozick doesn't use the term "gender binary," but her description of Jewish law's treatment of male and female as "complementary halves of a whole with little overlap between them" sounds very much like a description of the gender binary (124). See Ozick, "Notes Toward Finding the Right Question," 120–151.

12. However, the Mishnah and Talmud go to great lengths to define which women are allowed to marry Levites and Kohanim, recognizing that even within a patriarchal society, when it comes to marriage, women do count. See, for example, Mishnah Yevamot 10.

13. Unlike the Talmud, the Torah does not recognize that some people are intersex, with bodies that do not fit binary categories. However, it does recognize the existence of eunuchs, neutered males, who often held positions of responsibility in Iron Age societies.

14. United States Census Bureau, "Age and Sex: About," December 5, 2016. www.census.gov/topics/population/age-and-sex/about.html.

15. Gender surveillance can be so dangerous for transgender people that, as I mentioned in chapter 2, the therapist who helped me through gender transition instructed me to always carry a letter addressed "To whom it may concern," in which she assured whoever read it that I was not presenting myself as a woman in order to defraud or harm others.

16. Neither the Talmud's discussion of intersex Jews nor later Jewish law allows intersex Jews to define or identify themselves in terms of gender—to identify, for example, as transsexuals do, as men or women regardless of their physical sex. Like rules that govern Levites recorded as male, the rules governing intersex Jews are based on how their bodies appear to others, not on how they think about or understand themselves. For a medically and socially dated but useful summary of these rules, see Rabbi Alfred Cohen, "Tumtum and Androgynous," *Journal of Halacha & Contemporary Society* XXXVIII (Fall 1999). www.daat.ac.il/daat/english /journal/cohen-1.htm.

17. Even though it is God's idea that Abraham should leave his father's house, it is Abraham who decides to follow God's command.

18. In a sense, the Nazirite laws reverse the identity-altering dynamic we saw in God's relationship with Abraham. There, God tells Abraham to abandon his assigned gender role for the sake of a relationship with God. Here, God accepts that individuals may want to do so, even when God does not require it of them. But in both cases, the individual relationship with God offers a path beyond socially assigned roles.

19. Unlike transgender identities, one could, according to the rabbis, become a Nazirite accidentally. Mishnah Nazir 1 offers a number of casual expressions that would render one a Nazirite: "All colloquial terms for *nezirut* [a vow to forswear—for at least thirty days—grape products, corpse impurity, and cutting one's hair] are the same as *nezirut* [itself]. One who says, 'I will be,' is a Nazirite. Or, 'I will be beautiful,' is a Nazirite. 'Nazik,' 'naziach,' 'paziach,' he is a Nazirite. 'I am like this one,' 'I am to curl my hair,' 'I am to allow my hair to endure,' 'It is upon me to let it remain unbound,' he is a Nazirite. 'It is upon me [to offer] birds,' Rabbi Meir says: he is a Nazirite. The sages say: he is not a Nazirite" (Mishnah Nazir 1:1). Translations of passages from the Mishnah are based on *The Mishnah: A New Translation*, trans. Jacob Neusner (New Haven, CT: Yale University Press, 1991).

20. In a later verse, the Torah pragmatically recognizes that despite divine law, patriarchal power may trump women's power of self-determination, and that men may prevent women under their control from fulfilling their vows even after the period in which they had veto power has past. In such cases, the Torah tells us, men who unlawfully prevent women from fulfilling their vows will "bear the iniquity" that would otherwise fall on the vow breakers (Num. 30:15).

21. There is less emphasis on binaries in the Haggadah, the text that is read during the ritual meals that mark the beginning of the festival. There, binary oppositions such as slavery/freedom are surrounded by non-binary numbers, counting songs, and numerical delineations of categories, miracles, and events, multiplying the sense of complexity and wonder.

22. The Torah makes it clear that the commandment of circumcision that God gave to Abraham and his descendants does not define Israelite

identity. For example, the plague of the firstborn apparently struck circumcised males in households that were not marked with blood, and the mass circumcision led by Joshua upon entering Canaan shows that even Moses did not see circumcision as essential to Israelite identity.

23. Jacob was given the name "Israel" by the angelic opponent with whom he wrestled the night before his reunion with his brother Esau (Gen. 32:25–29), a name by which his descendants, the "children of Israel" or "Israelites," are often known.

24. Moses doesn't seem to consider himself a Midianite (he named their son Gershom, "stranger there," to express his own sense of being "a stranger in a foreign land"), but the Torah says nothing to indicate whether he still considered himself an Egyptian, or ever told his wife or adopted family that he was an Israelite (Exod. 2:21–22).

25. The non-binary category of leaven that is and isn't in our possession is further expanded by rules allowing Jews to temporarily transfer ownership of leaven that remains in our homes to non-Jews during Passover, so that we are legally not considered to possess that leaven even though we never actually remove it.

26. That basic law of Passover—"whoever eats what is leavened . . . shall be cut off from the community of Israel" (Exod. 12:19)—not only puts individual identities at risk; it also undermines the binary definition of Israelite identity. Israelites who eat leaven during Passover are still children of Israel in terms of lineage, family, and culture, but according to this law, they are no longer considered part of the Israelite community, and, thus, in crucial ways, are no longer considered Israelites. In other words, this law creates a non-binary category of people who both are and are not Israelites.

27. Whether we interpret *gerim* as referring to "resident aliens," as I have here, or as non-Israelites who have converted to the religion, it is clear that the Torah is complicating the Israelite/non-Israelite binary. I discuss *gerim* at greater length in the next chapter.

28. God's paradoxical relation to the Israelite/non-Israelite binary—simultaneously insisting on and undermining it—reminds me of my own can't-live-with-it, can't-live-without-it relation to binary gender. Without the binary category "female," I would have no way to name my own gender identification, and without binary conventions of gender expression,

I would have no way to express my gender identity to others. But when I—someone born and raised male—present myself as female, I confound the binary definition of female, much as participation in the Passover sacrifice by those who were considered strangers confounded the binary definition of Israelite.

29. Even today, Jews and Jewish communities around the world are subject to antisemitic attacks. Those attacks are only possible when Jews can be identified as Jews and distinguished from non-Jews. On the one hand, a clear, simple definition of Jewish identity enables Jewish communities to band together for support; on the other, as the beginning of Exodus reminds us, Jewish identity can easily be weaponized. The Exodus only happens because a pharaoh decided that no matter how long Israelites lived in Egypt, and no matter how much they contributed to the culture, there was an absolute distinction between Israelites and Egyptians that made Israelites untrustworthy, disloyal, and dangerous. That distinction became the basis for the enslavement in Egypt, just as it has been the basis for antisemitic actions throughout history.

30. See Genesis Rabbah 68:9. Translations of passages from Genesis Rabbah are based on *Midrash Rabbah*, ed. Freedman and Simon.

31. Of course, as I discuss in the next chapter, transgender people are far from the only people who know how it feels not to fit into the communities we live in, or to make sense in terms of categories that define others' identities and lives. But for transgender people wondering how traditional religions might speak to our lives, and for religious communities wondering what including transgender people and perspectives might contribute to religious traditions, it is important to recognize that the very differences that can make it so hard for trans people to fit in can also be a source of spiritual insight.

FIVE *Knowing the Soul of the Stranger*

1. As is often noted, the Haggadah—the text that is the basis for the ritual retelling of the Exodus at the Passover seder—mentions only God when recounting the Exodus, and does not mention Moses at all. When we juxtapose the Haggadah's version of the story with the Israelites' revi-

sionist history at Sinai, it looks as though later tradition is responding to the Israelites' amnesia about God by telling the story in a way that prevents later generations from making the same mistake.

2. The First and Second Temples were designed by human beings, built through taxes and forced labor, and represented the power of the state as well as devotion to God. The Tabernacle was a joint effort, designed by God and built through the generosity of the Israelites, who willingly contributed materials and labor in order to give God a place among them.

3. Abraham Joshua Heschel's *The Prophets* eloquently and exhaustively explores the repeated failures of God to find a place in Israelite society, and of Israelites to recognize and be faithful to the fact that God is there. Like God and the prophets, Heschel gives little consideration to any difficulties the Israelites might have had in relating to God. See Abraham Joshua Heschel, *The Prophets* (New York: Harper & Row, 1962).

4. W. E. B. Du Bois, *The Souls of Black Folk*, *The Journal of Pan African Studies* (New York: Penguin, 2002).

5. The comments Du Bois offers as examples of how white people talk to him are specific to his time and situation, but they also suggest the social difficulties that hyper-minorities and communities often have to navigate. The white people who flutter around Du Bois want to show him that they aren't racist: that they can consider a "colored man" to be "excellent," that they fought on the Union side in the Civil War, that they oppose white Southern efforts to destroy Reconstruction and terrorize black communities. They also want him to know that even though they see him as different in terms of race, they, like him, have feelings and experiences about race that they think he would share. But those comments also show that when they look at Du Bois, they can't help thinking about the color of his skin and how that makes him different from them, so different that it is hard for them to think or talk about anything else when they see him. I often find myself in a similar position, in which non-transgender people make supportive but irrelevant comments to me about transgender people they know or have heard of—comments that show they can't stop thinking about how I am different, and don't know how to talk with me about it.

God does not provoke comments like these in the Torah, because God is too different to socialize or make small talk. But one hopes that if the

Israelites had socialized with God, they would have known better than to refer sympathetically to other deities of their acquaintance.

6. I don't want to imply that people of color and transgender people face the same struggles, or to equate Du Bois's life as a pioneering African American intellectual and activist with my personal struggles. Being openly transgender in the Jewish world in the early twenty-first century is not at all like being a black intellectual and activist in America 115 years ago. But when I read Du Bois's description of the isolation and social awkwardness that go with being a hyper-minority, I feel a deep sense of familiarity and recognition—and because Du Bois writes his description without marking himself as black or his interlocutors as white, I suspect that he hoped that even readers who were not black would, like me, identify with his situation, despite our awareness of how different our lives are from his.

7. Du Bois, *Souls of Black Folk*, 6.

8. I am speaking here only of the way Du Bois portrays himself in the above paragraph. In his life, Du Bois was a fierce, courageous activist who fought for decades to empower African Americans and to tear down the veil that kept white people safe from knowing African American experiences, perspectives, and feelings.

9. In describing God as having human feelings such as anger, the Torah, as Maimonides argues, anthropomorphizes God. But here, it also seems that God wants the Israelites to understand the plague as an expression of "the anger of the LORD" rather than, say, as the kind of judgment Abraham sees God as exercising when God destroys Sodom and Gomorrah. God *does* seem to be judging and punishing the Israelites, but the sin for which they are being punished—is it being dissatisfied with the life God has given them? speaking fondly of their lives in Egypt? gluttony?—is not clear. What *is* clear, both in the Torah's telling and presumably to the Israelites, is that God is angry with them. Read from this perspective, "the anger of the LORD" is not just an anthropomorphic phrase but an act of social *tzimtzum*, an example of God acting in ways that make God's presence visible and intelligible to human beings—in this case, by emphasizing that, as Moses and the prophets repeatedly say, God not only judges communal Israelite behavior but also responds to it personally, emotionally, and with what Heschel calls "divine *pathos*." See Heschel, *The Prophets*, 29.

10. In the Torah's telling, the problem in God's relationships with humanity is never God: it is the refusal of human beings, like the Israelites during their rebellions and Pharaoh during the plagues, to accommodate God's feelings and demands. We see a similar perspective in many texts by and in support of transgender people. They present the moral necessity of accommodating trans identities as obvious, and rarely address the concerns or qualms of those whose lives are affected by those accommodations.

11. Although God has a hard time getting along with the Israelite community, when it comes to relationships with individuals, God's demands are generally accommodated. It's unlikely that Abraham is happy about abandoning his elderly father, and Moses makes it quite clear at the burning bush that he prefers to return to his life as a shepherd rather than help God lead the Israelites out of Egypt, but both of them change their lives in the way God wants them to. That can be the case for hyper-minorities, too: we often find individuals in our communities who are ready to accommodate our differences even when our communities as a whole are not.

12. By saying "openly transgender people," I am referring to people who want others to know that we don't fit binary gender categories. That excludes trans people who, like me when I lived as a man, do not want others to know that we are transgender, as well as transsexuals who, after gender transition, want to be seen not as transgender but as men or women.

13. When people are called up during the public reading of the Torah at religious services, they are named, in Hebrew, as "X [their Hebrew first name], son or daughter of Y [the Hebrew names of their parents]."

14. Although the new JPS translation renders this as "you know the *feelings* of the stranger"—a translation that captures the colloquial meaning of the text—the Hebrew word is actually *nefesh*, "soul."

15. The Torah not only reports that Miriam and Aaron referred to Tzipporah as "a Cushite woman"; it too uses that phrase to describe her, reinforcing the idea that this is how she is generally known among the Israelites.

16. Other Israelites should know this too, if only because Tzipporah's father Jethro spends time as an honored guest in their community after the Exodus.

17. Because Cushites were identified with dark skin, the phrase "Cushite woman" may have been drawing attention to that difference as well. Ancient

Israelites did not have the kind of system of racial discrimination that we see in the United States today, and it is impossible to tell from the Torah whether referring to Tzipporah as a Cushite woman is identifying her as different in terms of ethnicity, skin color, or both.

18. There are a number of rabbinic commentaries that interpret the reference to Tzipporah as a Cushite woman as praise rather than disparagement. For example, Midrash Tanhuma Zav 13 explains that Tzipporah is referred to as a Cushite because the numerical value of "Kushit" (fem. Cushite) is equal to *yafet mareh* ("beautiful"); Talmud Bavli Moed Katan 16b says: "But is her name Cushite? Tzipporah is her name! Rather, just as a Cushite is distinguished by his [dark] skin, so too, Tzipporah was distinguished by her actions."

Such commentaries show that whatever Tzipporah's position among the Israelites, later tradition embraces and valorizes her. However, commentators' strained efforts to interpret "Cushite" as a reference to Tzipporah's beauty or virtue show that they were aware that in this Torah passage, "Cushite" sounds like an epithet.

19. The phrase "the stranger who dwells among you" makes explicit the connotations of the word *ger*, which is derived from a root that means "to dwell."

20. Although the Israelites were not hyper-minorities in the land of Egypt—there were a lot of them—the term *ger* includes people who are hyper-minorities, because hyper-minorities are those who, like me at my university, are seen as too different to fit in by a community that we consider our own.

21. I discuss the connection between the laws of the first Passover and Israelite identity at the end of chapter 4.

22. This passage implicitly distinguishes between two kinds of *gerim*: the uncircumcised *ger*, who dwells among Israelites but is not sufficiently committed to the community of Israel to be circumcised; and the *ger* who identifies so strongly with the Israelites that he circumcises himself and all males in his household and is not only allowed to participate in the Passover offering but is also considered to be like a citizen of the country. (Because of the focus on circumcision, this passage only addresses *gerim* who are male.)

23. I have no doubt that this don't-ask-don't-tell policy is intended to protect people who convert to Judaism against being shamed and gossiped about. In that regard, it represents an institutional attempt to know the soul of the stranger by anticipating and guarding against some of the verbal violence, intentional or not, to which they may be subjected. But, as I have found at my university, where an unofficial version of this rule keeps people from mentioning that I am transgender, silencing discussion of the ways in which members of communities are different ends up hardening the idea that we are strangers whose feelings and experiences can never be known or understood. Prohibitions against acknowledging differences isolate those who are seen as *gerim* and deprive our communities of being enriched by our differences: we are sources of social discomfort (or, as Du Bois, might say, problems) rather than sources of new thinking, insight, and discovery. In short, this effort to protect those who are seen as strangers ends up making it impossible for us to know the soul of the stranger—and thus to recognize what we have in common with those we see as strangers.

24. For more on the treatment of the *ger tzedek*, see, for example, Talmud Bavli Bava Metzia 58b–59b.

25. Because Jews have not generally sought to convert others to Judaism, most Jews who convert are in the position of being hyper-minorities—not only being seen as different from other Jews in their community, as *gerim*, but also being among a few who are different the way they are different.

26. Although I now worry about and occasionally experience harassment for being seen as transgender, as before, my white skin enables me to walk through the world without being marked for discrimination or police attention.

27. It is important to note that, contrary to the assumption built into the term *ger tzedek*, neither all Jews who have converted nor all transgender people are seen as strangers in their communities. Communities *can* embrace those who are different as *us*, though I suspect most communities find this harder to do with regard to members who are visibly different, like Tzipporah, or trans people whose appearances don't fit binary norms.

I explore the parallels between gender transition and Jewish conversion in "How We Become Real: The Making of Jewish and Transsexual Identities," *Journal of Jewish Identities*.

INDEX

gender failure: author's experience of, 48; as common experience, 47–48; Sarah's infertility as, 46–48

gender identities: as always a compromise, 2–3, 7; as different in different circumstances, 35–36, 152–53n2; as social convention, 18; variations over time and place, 24. *See also* patriarchal system

gender identities, binary: author's complex relation to, 73–74; as basis of most social relationships, 3, 100–101; citing of Genesis as evidence for, 19, 30, 33–34; defining of social responsibilities by, 58; as feature of all cultures, 24, 150n1; flexibility of, as issue, 121; as given in most religions, 4, 7; history of, 16; isolation of those outside, 25; life-long wounds inflicted by, 56; roles assigned by, 16; as oppressive to many, 17, 25, 56, 101–2, 157n28; options for accommodating transgender persons, 121; as oversimplification, 24–25; parallels to Passover laws, 117, 119–21, 168–69n28; as promises of stable identity, 83; and surgical "correction" of intersex newborns, 151n9; useful social functions of, 17–18, 121. *See also* binaries

gender identities, in Torah: as absolute and unquestioned, 96–99, 113; author's selective application of laws related to, 93–94; complexity of, 30; as destiny, 98, 101–2, 107–8; God's uses and disruptions of,

57–58, 156n22; human rather than divine origin of, 97; as secondary to human identity, in Genesis, 31, 32–33. *See also* Genesis creation story; Levite census commandments

gender surveillance, 102–3, 166n15

Genesis creation story: Adam's invention of gender, 27, 31, 32; and benefits of binary gender, 28; and common humanity of man and woman, 26–27; creation of Adam and Eve, 25–27; equality of genders in, 28; fluidity of gender identities in, 32; gender binary of Adam and Eve as not universal, 30; God's limited interest in binary gender in, 33, 151–52n10; humanity as prior to gender in, 31, 32–33; and humans as image of God, 33–34; initial creation of sexes, not genders, 20–21, 25–26; male focus of, 28; origin of patriarchal system in curse of original sin, 28–30; reading implying androgyny of first human being, 150–51n5; Trible's depatriarchalizing reading of, 151–52n10; use as evidence for binary gender, 19, 30, 33–34; use of binaries in, 21–23, 27–28

gerim (strangers; resident aliens): definition of, 141–42, 173n19; as familiar experience for many, 145–46; as forever strangers, 143; *ger tzedek* (righteous stranger), Rabbinic laws protecting, 143, 174n23; God as, 146–47; God's command to empathize with,

suppressed discussion of difference, 174n23; as last-ditch effort to express true identity, 46; long-time inability to imagine, 49, 50–51; and loss of custody of children, 104; and loss of friends, 58, 144; as self-centered act of becoming, 43–44, 45–46, 110–11; teaching position and, 58, 72, 104, 105, 106, 134–35, 174n23; and white privilege, 174n26

Maimonides, Moses: on God's name, 163n25; on God's nature, 66–68, 73, 77, 86, 97, 146, 159–60nn6–8; on human language and assumptions in Torah, 97, 165n6; on importance of education about God's nature, 158–59n5; on language's inability to describe God, 67, 86, 159–60nn7–8; on language's over-generalization, 87; on portrayals of God, 161–62n14; views on gender, 158n4
males, Jewish, privileges of, 143–44
Meyerowitz, Joanne, 24
Moses: as both Israelite and Egyptian, 114–16; and circumcision, 167–68n22; desire to avoid God-given mission, 115; and Exodus, 124–25, 126, 127, 128, 133, 169n1; and expulsion of Israelites with eruptions or discharges, 103–4, 105; God's appearances to, 71, 84–85, 87–88, 89–91; and God's self-naming, 87–88, 89–91, 164nn25–27; on placing God at center of Israelite community, 129; and prohibition on cross-dressing,

94–95, 102, 105, 165n8; and Ten Commandments, 75, 84–85; wife of, as ger (resident alien), 139–40

Nahman, Rabbi, 48
Nazirite vows, 108–10; balance of women's and patriarchal rights in, 111–12, 167n20; behavioral restrictions in, 108; casual expressions equivalent to, 167n19; as open to both women and men, 108; parallels to gender transition, 108–10, 111–12; as path beyond assigned social roles, 167n18
negative theology, 66–68, 158–59nn5–6
Numbers' census commandments. See Levite census commandments

Ozick, Cynthia, 99, 166n11

parents and family of author: camping trip with, 63–64; father's funeral, inability to attend, 104; fear of rejection by, 2, 25, 38–39, 92, 94, 103, 117, 140; love for author's male persona, 2, 125, 126; mother's acceptance of transition, 104; and Passover, 116–17; rejection of queer men by, 140–41
Passover, 113–22; ambiguous starting point of, 117; author's parents' observance of, 116–17; and kitniyot rules, 118; laws on (Exodus), 113–14; as remembrance of Israelites ger (stranger) status, 147
Passover, binary distinctions asserted

complete integration of God into community in Torah, 127, 170n2; and otherness of God, 130

Talmud: on intersex Jews, 19–20, 105–6, 151n9, 166n16; on *mashal l'melech basar v'dam*, 150n5; on Sarah's gender failure, 48, 154–55n18

Ten Commandments, handing down of: God's delivery in human language, 163n23; God's direct address to Israelites in, 123–24; and God's insistence on recognition of God's otherness in, 125–26; God's spectacular appearance during, 84–85; and Israelites' difficulty in relating to God, 75; and Israelites' turn to idol worship, 163n23

Torah: author's rejection of gender-based laws in, 93–94; cultural assumptions in, 97, 165n6; gender surveillance in, 102; as lifelong comfort to author, 15, 60; ongoing influence on author, 96; patriarchal perspective of, 97; threat of violence in, as evocative of author's childhood fears, 92; as tree of life, 15, 96. *See also* gender identities, in Torah; *other specific topics*

Torah, sparse style of: echo of author's dissociated self in, 92; and focus on moments of God's presence, 95–96

Torah interpretation: author's standards for, 11–12; Jewish tradition on, 10–11; and *pshat* (plain sense) of text, 11

Torah's relevance to transgender experience, 96; illumination of,

as goal, 10; and Jewish exegetical tradition, 10–11; and silence on transgender persons, 96–97, 99, 105, 106

trans experiences in Torah, 35; author's childhood failure to recognize, 71; author's focus on, after transition, 72; and God's disregard for assigned gender roles, 57–58; and *mashal l'melech basar v'dam*, 150n5; most people's ability to empathize with, 35–36. *See also* Abraham; Akedah; Hagar; Ishmael; Jacob; Sarah

transgender, as term, 9, 86

transgender identity: and communication as compromise of, 86–87; discomfort with, 133–35, 170n5, 171n6; future acceptance of, 7; as inherently secular, 3; and ostracization, 31; and prioritization of self-identification, 107

transgender identity, opponents of: characterizations of transgender persons, 19, 110–11, 153n6; citing of Genesis creation story, 19, 30, 33–34

transgender identity, supporters of: focus on individual's happiness, 110

transgender identity of author: change over time in, 9–10; childhood belief in sinfulness of, 94–95; childhood suffering from, 78, 81; closeness to God resulting from, 3, 70, 71, 72, 93; comfort derived from God's disregard of binary gender, 58; in early childhood, 17; fear of revealing, 2, 25, 61–63, 67–68, 87,